Freshman Year of Life

D0954157

Freshman Year of Life

ESSAYS THAT TELL THE TRUTH

ABOUT WORK, HOME, AND LOVE

AFTER COLLEGE

Conceived by the
MindSumo community

FLATIRON
BOOKS
NEW YORK

The following pieces were previously published and may appear in a slightly different form in this book:
"A Story of a Fuck Off Fund" by Paulette Perhach was originally published on TheBillfold.com on January 20, 2016.
"Outsider/Insider" by Jenny Zhang was originally published in *Rookie* magazine on April 18, 2012.
"Everything Is Fine" by Jamie Lauren Keiles was originally published on NYMag.com/TheCut on January 14, 2016.
"Why I Want to Live Like I'm Forty in my Twenties" by Ashley Ford was originally published on TueNight.com on March 3, 2015.
"How to Make New Friends as an Adult and Why" by Puja Patel was originally published on Deadspin.com on October 28, 2015.

The Library of Congress Cataloging-in-Publication Data is available upon request.

ISBN 978-1-250-07118-7 (trade paperback)
ISBN 978-1-250-07119-4 (e-book)

Our books may be purchased in bulk for promotional, educational, or business use. Please contact your local bookseller or the Macmillan Corporate and Premium Sales Department at 1-800-221-7945, extension 5442, or by e-mail at MacmillanSpecialMarkets@macmillan.com.

First Edition: April 2017

10 9 8 7 6 5 4 3 2 1

*To everyone navigating
their freshman year of life*

We know what we are, but not what we may be.
—WILLIAM SHAKESPEARE

Contents

→←

PART 2

Home and Belonging

PART 3
Love and Relationships

Introduction

illions of books, blog posts, personal essays, and advice columns are written about college, but what about after college? Those first few years of finding your footing in the real world are filled with transitional crises and fraught introspection. You're a freshman all over again.

The thirty-eight essays in *Freshman Year of Life* tell the truth about life beyond college graduation from the voices of people a few years out. Some of their stories are funny, some heartwarming; some are about their successes, and others reflect their failures. There are stories about going from a committed college relationship to casual dating in an unfamiliar city, navigating a toxic work environment, learning how to stay patient in a part of your life that isn't defined by semesters and finals, and tackling the task of making new friends, something you may not have had to do since college orientation.

Freshman Year of Life includes writers with large followings, but we didn't want to only hear from people with big platforms. That's where MindSumo comes in. The MindSumo community of college students and recent graduates came up with the idea for this book. We asked them what book they would most like to have available to them upon graduation, and they overwhelmingly responded with requests for authentic essays from people like themselves. And so we went back into that community to hear stories from people just like you. That's why this book includes words from people who have millions of followers and some you haven't heard of . . . yet.

Even with thirty-eight voices, this doesn't begin to scratch the surface. There are a multitude of different experiences out there, and one of them will be your own. It's not the end of the conversation; it's the start.

PART ONE

→←

Work and Money

The Extra Mile(s)

→» «←

ALANA MASSEY

French is the only official foreign language I speak according to my résumé, but I am also fluent in the rarer and more mysterious tongue of job boards. Littered with platitudes and euphemisms and code words for unforeseen labor, they all demand just a little more than they appear to and cloak these demands in requests for good attitudes. As I would come to learn in May of 2007 when I was fresh off a B.A. in history from NYU, entry-level roles are especially susceptible to being written deceptively. I applied to countless administrative and junior roles after ticking off the requisite Microsoft and Adobe programs and the basic computer skills I'd had since childhood. But following all of these hard and fast skills were qualifications like "Ready to do what it takes to get the job done," "Willing to go the extra mile for their team," and the rather ominous "Clock-watchers need not apply."

I became the executive assistant to the CEO of a successful snack food enterprise *and* a burgeoning nonprofit with three international offices and hugely ambitious plans for expansion the year I joined. I dove headlong into calendar and e-mail management, foolishly believing that the kind of man who could both ascend to power in the cutthroat world of gourmet snacks and make a name for himself in philanthropy could be tamed by my meek attempts to quell his entrepreneurial spirit for long enough to make conference calls on time. My polite reminders in Outlook and my timid knocks at his office door while he was bellowing into the phone went largely ignored.

While he brushed off my attempts to perform my basic duties, he sent long late-night e-mails elaborating his plans to start a blog that I would serve as ghostwriter for. *I am ready to do what it takes to get the job done.* One night he demanded that the communications director and I renegotiate the price of the lapel pins of our logo with a manufacturer in China on the eve of an important national holiday there and well after midnight in our offices. *I will not be a clock-watcher, I will not be a clock-watcher.* I was flattered by his confidence that I could handle roles beyond the administrative ones for which I was hired as I scripted public service announcements for A-list celebrity speakers and managed production from across the country. *I am going the extra mile.*

After three months, my provisional status was supposed to come under review and move me from contract employee to full-time. My boss rescheduled the meeting three times before finally calling me in his office to discuss my progress. Instead of letting me summarize my accomplishments, he gave a hasty little speech on how he wanted to watch my performance in the lead-up to a big event before committing to taking me on full-time. I swear on my mother's good name, he *winked* at me as he delivered this verdict. Floored by his failure to see the value of my labor but obstinate in my need to prove myself, I threw myself into more work. I went miles beyond the extra miles. I did what it took. I kept my eyes off the clock and not just because I could hardly keep them open by the time I left the office.

On a Saturday night, I had a friend over for drinks, and when my boss called my cell phone after midnight, I reflexively jumped away from the phone. I burst into tears at seeing his name flash across the display and stood away from it, as if he might peer out of the screen to see me momentarily enjoying myself and scorn me accordingly when we were face-to-face again. It took being witnessed by outside observers to realize the extent to which I'd let myself be consumed and defeated in the effort to prove I was ready to do what it takes.

I quit the following week. My boss dramatically begged me to stay, even initially refusing my resignation. Rather than his usual custom of simply shouting me into his office when he wanted to talk, he sent me calendar invites to discuss how we might make the role work for me. He recited a litany of the vital things I offered the office for much of the time we'd allotted for the meeting. I sat politely and listened attentively despite my now unflinching resolve to leave. I watched the clock behind him strike 5:00 P.M., the end time of our meeting, and stood to leave. I thanked him for the opportunity and headed out the door, traveling no more and no less than the 2.1 miles it took on my bike to get me from the office back home.

What isn't immediately apparent about those personality traits listed in job descriptions is that they are designed to be self-perpetuating. Once you do what it takes the first time, you're groomed to do even more the next time. And the first extra mile is just the first leg of the race. If you're willing to go the extra mile often enough, you find yourself lost and alone, so focused on the task at hand that you've forgotten where the clocks are, even if you wanted to watch them. These descriptions are meant to flatter young people who will agree that they are the tenacious types who roll up their sleeves and prove themselves, which is just a rosy way to describe the extraction of labor from a person without paying fairly for it.

The irony, of course, is that the same tenacity that kept me in the office for those endless, uncompensated hours was what enabled me to leave the job when I realized that my boundaries and labor were being disrespected. And it is that same tenacity that soon got me a new job that was advertised with the skills it required rather than the personal demands it would exert. My new employer respected my labor there, and for what it's worth, they had a clock waiting for me right on my desk.

Stepping-Stones

→←

ALISON GILBERT

M y college choice was born of secondhand nostalgia from hearing stories of my mother's time at the George Washington University during the early '70s in Washington, D.C. Watching *Forrest Gump* as a kid and then hearing these stories, I wanted to live out my romanticized idea of being part of a historical moment and joining the equivalent of the hippie subculture of my time. My college choice was entirely based on gut, whim, fantasy.

When I had to choose my major, I chose English. I didn't like taking tests, and I grew up doing better in the language arts and humanities. My gut told me this would be a suitable choice and transferable to pursuing law. I had decided even before I began college that law school was next after graduation. If I wasn't going to be the Jewish doctor I thought my parents wanted me to be, I would be the Jewish lawyer.

After finishing at GW, with two rounds of LSAT test taking under my belt and a list of law schools to apply to, I struggled to hammer out the personal statement. I shared my writing troubles with a friend, who asked me what the prompt was. "Why do you want to be a lawyer?" I told him.

After a pause, he replied, "Alison, if you're having trouble answering that question, then maybe you need to rethink what you're doing next."

Up until this moment in my life, I skipped from one life choice to the next, with a "well, why not, that seems right" attitude. But deciding to not go to law school felt big. It was the first time life and intuition were actively telling me if I didn't dig in and figure it out, I would not be happy moving forward.

No anecdote nor ism can capture the inner push and pull I felt in coming to terms with not going. If I was not Alison, the girl on the path to pursuing law and a career that fulfilled society's idea of a smart person grooming herself to be a successful adult, then who was I?

But once I decided not to go, my world unfolded in a series of stepping-stones that seemed to just appear as I went from one job to the next. Cooking and baking had been a go-to pastime throughout my life—preparing weeknight dinners for my family growing up, tinkering with different pastry recipes for all the holidays, procrastinating from law school essay writing by baking peach cobblers and berry crisps.

I answered a Craigslist ad to be a baker at a just-opened-up bakery in my Jersey Shore hometown. I was offered the job and took it. That turned into my managing that bakery. From there, I was sparked to follow my baking passion further. I enrolled in culinary school and moved to New York. Fast-forward to being in the right place at the right time, I got a part-time assistant job at a brand-new food magazine startup called Tasting Table. Having grown up spectating the food media world, watching cooking celebrities on food TV channels after school and reading about recipes in magazines like racy novels, I had ended up in that world myself.

Then I got offered an opportunity to run my own bakery back in New Jersey, and I said yes. I kept the part-time assistant job (it didn't hurt to have a backup plan), but packed all my belongings up, and headed back to Jersey, only to pull into my parents' driveway and realize, *Wait, this doesn't feel right.* For what reason, I didn't know. It just didn't. My gut was telling me. I turned right around, moved back into the city (I had not yet found a sublet for my apartment), and a week later the CEO at Tasting Table gave me a full-time job.

I'd gone from working in a pastry kitchen to eventually becoming chief operating officer at Tasting Table, all because I let go of my plan and listened to my gut instead. I discovered a new passion for growing businesses, and after helping build Tasting Table into a forty-person, multimillion-dollar company with readership in the millions, I went on to start my own business consulting company. And I did it all not because of what others wanted and what was expected of me, but because I followed what I wanted.

I would never have been able to plan all these stepping-stones out from the beginning. The hardest part was and still is figuring out how to create the space in my brain to listen to my gut. But I work at it every day because I'm excited about where my gut is taking me. I'm excited to see where I'm taking myself.

A Story of a Fuck Off Fund

→» «←

PAULETTE PERHACH

You're telling your own story: You graduated college and you're a grown-ass woman now. Tina Fey is your hero; Beyoncé, your preacher.

You know how to take care of you. You've learned self-defense. If any man ever hit you, you'd rip his eyes out. You've seen *Mad Men*, and if anyone ever sexually harassed you at work, you'd tell him to fuck right off, throw your coffee in his face, and wave two middle fingers as you marched out the door.

You get your first internship. You get your first credit card. You get to walk into Nordstrom, where your mom would never take you, and congratulate yourself with one fabulous black leather skirt, and the heels to match.

Your car? It's the car of a college student. You get a lease, graduate from the rusted Civic to last year's Accord.

You get your first student loan bill, and look at all those numbers.

Your life turns into a stock photo tagged "young professionals": you and your new work friends, hanging out at the bar across the street from the office. The cocktails cost twice as much as you paid when you still measured time by semesters and nights by cans of PBR.

The college boyfriend gets serious. You move into his place, spruce it up by buying your first coffee table together. IKEA lets you put half on your newest credit card.

Your internship ends before you find a permanent job. You pay minimum payments, then max out your cards again buying two days' worth of groceries and filling your gas tank halfway.

Your bank app upgrades to a new feature that combines all your balances—the shiny Nordstrom card with the Visa and the Chase Freedom you were only supposed to use for emergencies—and tells you that somehow you owe people $7,000.

Your boyfriend offers to cover the rent for a while. You get a job a few months later, but you're that many loan payments behind. Your first paycheck feels like a breath of air that gets sucked right out of your lungs.

Your new boss, who seems nice, calls you in his office, shows you a picture of his kids. He jokes about his son, then as you're laughing, he puts his hand on your arm, gives you a little squeeze. You smile it off.

You wait to pay the electric bill while you're gathering up the half you owe, and the lights go out. On your phone you see the e-mail about the fifty dollar late fee. Your boyfriend asks how you could be so stupid. "I am not stupid," you say. You would never be with someone who called you names, but you would never be able to make first, last, and deposit right now, either.

You say yes to payday P. F. Chang's with your new coworkers, because you want to make friends, your turkey sandwich sounds boring, and what's one more charge? You buy a halter dress you know you can't afford, because it makes you look like the successful young woman you want everyone to think you are.

Your boss tells you that you look nice in that dress, asks you to do a spin. Just to get the moment over with, you do.

Your boyfriend asks you how much you paid for it, says it makes you look chubby. You lock yourself in the bathroom until he bangs on the door so hard you think he must have hurt himself. After he falls asleep, you search Craigslist for places, and can't believe how expensive rent's gotten around town. You erase your Internet history and go to sleep.

A few weeks later, your boss calls a one-on-one in his office, walks up behind you, and stands too close. His breath fogs your neck. His hand crawls up your new dress. You squirm away. He says, "Sorry, I thought . . ."

You know what to do. You're just shocked to find you're not doing it. You are not telling him to fuck off. You are not storming out. All you're doing is math. You have $159 in the bank and your car payment and your maxed-out credit cards and you'll die before you ask your dad for a loan again and it all equals one thought: *I need this job.*

"It's okay," you hear your voice saying. "Just forget it." You scurry out of the room, survey the office half full of women, and wonder how many of them have secrets like the one you're about to keep.

At the apartment, your best guy friend calls. After you hang up, your boyfriend says you laugh too much with him, that you're flirting with him, probably sleeping with him. You say it's not like that. You yell, he yells. You try to leave, he blocks your way. When you struggle to get by, he grabs your wrist in the exact way they pretended to in self-defense class, and you know to go for the eyes, but you don't know how to go for his eyes. He yanks you back until you fall and crack the coffee table.

He seems so sorry, cries, even, so that night you lie down in the same bed. You stare up at the dark and try to calculate how long it would take you to save up the cash to move out. Telling yourself that he's sorry, convincing yourself it was an accident, discounting this one time because he didn't hit you, exactly, seems much more feasible than finding the money, with what you owe every month. The next time you go out as a couple, his arm around your shoulders, you look at all the other girlfriends and imagine finger-sized bruises under their long sleeves.

Wait. This story sucks. If it were one of those Choose Your Own Adventures, here's where you'd want to flip back, start over, rewrite what happens to you.

You graduated college and you're a grown-ass woman now. Tina Fey is your hero; Beyoncé, your preacher.

If any man ever hit you, if anyone ever sexually harassed you, you'd tell him to fuck right off. You want to be, no, you *will* be the kind of woman who can tell anyone to fuck off if a fuck off is deserved, so naturally you start a Fuck Off Fund.

To build this account, you keep living like you lived as a broke student. Drive the decade-old Civic even after the fender falls off. Buy the thrift store clothes. You waitress on Saturdays, even though you work Monday through Friday. You make do with the garage sale coffee table. It's hard, your loan payments suck, but you make girls' night an at-home thing and do tacos potluck.

You save up a Fuck Off Fund of $1,000, $2,000, $3,000, then enough to live half a year without anyone else's help. So when your boss tells you that you look nice, asks you to do a spin, you say, "Is there some way you need my assistance in the professional capacity or can I go back to my desk now?"

When your boyfriend calls you stupid, you say if he ever says that again, you're out of there, and it's not hard to imagine how you'll accomplish your getaway.

When your boss attempts to grope you, you say, "Fuck off, you creep!" You wave two middle fingers in the air, and march over to HR. Whether the system protects you or fails you, you will be able to take care of yourself.

When your boyfriend pounds the door, grabs your wrist, you see it as the red flag it is, leave a Post-it in the night that says, "Fuck off, lunatic douche!" You stay up in a fancy hotel drinking room service champagne, shopping for apartments, and swiping around on Tinder.

Once your Fuck Off Fund is built back up, with your new, better job, you pay cash for the most badass black leather skirt you can find, upgrade to the used but nicer convertible you've always wanted, and start saving to go to Thailand with your best friend the next summer.

Yes, that's a better story.

It's a story no one ever told me.

It's the kind I'd hope for you.

The Ass-Whooping of a Lifetime

→»«←

LINCOLN BLADES

I've had two real arguments with my mother. The first was after my university freshman tour and orientation. My mother and I went to the campus, looked around, asked many questions about the faculties, and then drove home—leading to the biggest fight we've ever had. Now, this isn't a story about my mother kicking my ass, although I have ducked a plastic racetrack before, but the fight we had was memorable not just because it was my first time screaming at her (something West Indian kids never dared to do to an adult) but also because I didn't really know what I was arguing. All I knew was that I didn't want to be there, and I couldn't feel if it was because I hated the school, hated the idea of going to university, or if I just felt generally unprepared for this massive life event in my potentially "perfect life." The only other time we argued anything close to that was when my parents ruled out the idea of me majoring in journalism ("What kind of broke-ass boy desires to grow up to be a broke-ass man? Not under this roof.").

I just knew that I wasn't ready for this, but you can't say that to your university-educated parents when checks have already been cashed and living arrangements organized. I hated the entire process with every inch of my soul, but not going to postsecondary school was not an option. That's what losers did, according to my parents.

After three years of school, I felt like I was done and ready to enter the real world. I knew what my professional field of choice was gonna be (finance), and right out of school I had a job lined up, and I was ready to go. For years I worked my ass off, got promotions, bought myself a luxury car, and began dating an attractive lawyer who was eager to settle down and have kids. With all that good shit going on, the chase of the potentially perfect life should've been over—but then it happened.

The ass-whooping of a lifetime.

One day, I came home exhausted from a twelve-hour shift at work, managing high-strung clients all day, and as soon as I opened the door and slammed it firmly behind me, something hard smashed me in the back of my skull. I felt my knees buckle, landing me in Catholic boy prayer position, and before I could even raise my palms to embrace the wound, my temples began throbbing like I caught a Georges St-Pierre knee to the side of my face. Now, I don't cry very easily (except when maybe the Raiders lose), but I felt the tears coming because I felt so damn helpless and my body was racked with pain. As I rolled onto my back, preparing to see the culprit, I blinked my eyes open and didn't see anyone there. The door chime didn't go off, and the house was completely silent, awakening me to the fact that no one was ever there, and the very real pain I felt that laid my ass out wasn't a burglar—it was completely internal and self-inflicted.

I had had a panic attack.

Yup, a big, grown, hardback man was trapped in a frenzy of fear, dismay, and anxiety. And I know exactly who the culprit was: Passion. I was working a "good" job I didn't like, dating a woman that was "good on paper" who I didn't love and who also called me silly for wanting to be a writer, and keeping up with the Joneses in every sense of the term when I truly didn't give a shit about impressing them.

My pursuit of the "perfect life" took me away from the thing that gave me purpose, carved my identity, and satiated my soul. I thought those were the needs of the artsy-fartsy who were incapable of making it in the professional world, but I was wrong. And here I stand, officially ten years removed from my last year of school as a full-time writer with a gorgeous, loving, and intelligent woman by my side who supports me in everything I do. The type of woman I couldn't have even dreamed existed. I've even made my parents proud in ways I never had before. The first seven years of my post-university life were dedicated to doing what I felt was expected of me, while repressing the most intrinsic parts of my being. I thought I was fast enough to outrun myself, but I was dead wrong.

The first year you truly set out into your adult life, the one you actually want to live, can begin anytime. Happily ever after is a terrible goal to aim for. There will be a time when things are going to be absolute shit, and that's just a natural part of life. But as long as you are armed with deep satisfaction about who you are and what you're doing, you will never truly be without hope—and you'll never have to worry about getting your ass jumped by Passion when you least expect it.

Wait for It

➔❮

CHLOE ANGYAL

About four months after I graduated from college, on a chilly autumn evening, I was venting my professional frustrations to a dear friend.

"I just feel like, we've been out of school for a while now and I'm still not . . ." I started.

"—an internationally renowned feminist writer?" Jordan finished.

"Yeah!" I said earnestly, not realizing that she was mocking me.

Jordan, who is barely older but much, much wiser than me, raised her eyebrows and looked at me, in all my genuine angst, and sat there waiting patiently for me to think about what I'd been about to say—waiting for me to realize how absurd it was.

In some situations, four months can be reasonably termed *a while*. If you are waiting for a person you just went on a date with to text you back, four months is a long while, and that person is either being very rude or in a coma. This was not one of those situations. Six years later, I'm still not internationally renowned (and I no longer aspire to be), though I have been fortunate enough to have some impact and, I hope, do some real good.

I've always been an impatient person. I was an impatient child and a very impatient young adult. When I got out of college, I wanted instant success, instant acclaim, instant impact. I was willing to work for it, but I was far less willing to wait for it. If it ever occurred to me that this was almost inherently paradoxical, I don't remember it.

And with impatience often comes its unpleasant bedfellow, arrogance. My first job out of college was as a part-time administrative assistant for a nonprofit organization with a wonderful mission that aligned perfectly with my own politics and my own desire to change the world. I was delighted to be working for a cause I believed in and to be surrounded by people who were, like me, dedicated to making the world a better place.

The only problem was that I was the world's worst administrative assistant. I was sloppy at following instructions and careless with details, and as excited as I was by the work of the organization, I was singularly uninterested in *my* work at the organization—the paying of bills, the filing of forms, the mailing of packages. I told myself that was because it wasn't interesting work, and it wasn't, but that's not why I was bad at it. I was bad at it because I thought it was beneath me. I had just graduated from a fancy school, and I knew all about the big issues the organization was tackling; I was meant for greater things, I told myself, than unchallenging administrative box-checking. When, after five months, I told my manager I was quitting and she frostily said, "I think that makes sense," I knew that she'd been planning to fire me, anyway.

Conventional wisdom would have it that my impatience and entitlement were a function of the generation in which I came of age. I'm not so sure. I don't think it was a matter of millennial entitlement, if that's even a thing, or if it's any more of a thing than boomer entitlement or flapper entitlement. I don't think we're living in a time of unprecedented impatience and arrogance in young people; young people have always wanted the world and wanted it *now*.

And it's okay to want that. It is okay to want to change the world and to feel an urgency about doing good—there is, after all, a great deal of good to be done. And there's nothing wrong with wanting to make something of yourself, and quickly; after all, you only live once, and you don't live for that long.

And there are some people who have become who they want to be, and had the impact they want to have, through impatience and arrogance. We, somewhat perversely, tend to lionize those people, the ones who buck the system and alienate people in service of great accomplishments and the greater good. That kind of story makes for a much better biopic than a script about those who maintained perspective, patiently waited, didn't entertain pretensions of grandeur, alienated no one, and accomplished, over time, what they wanted to achieve. If those stories do get told, they're usually dispensed with in a quick, compelling montage—which might partially explain my coexisting willingness to work hard and distaste for waiting.

It's particularly hard when you're fresh out of college to be patient and humble, in part because you're ushered off campus with soaring commencement rhetoric about how the world is yours to inherit, about how you're now equipped to change the world and to become someone great. Those well-intentioned exhortations can be accurate, but I wish my commencement speakers had told my graduating class that, as great as we were, as responsible as we were for tackling the great challenges of the world, we ought to resist the temptation to believe that the world should be instantly ours.

Few traits in life will serve you better—in your first year out of college, and every year after that—than patience and humility. Few things will make you a better leader, a better partner, a better friend, a better citizen, and even a better administrative assistant.

They're not traits we're all born with, but they can be cultivated, and that's a lifelong project for many of us. But if you're lucky, life will be long—shorter than you realize, but longer than you fear—and you'll have time to cultivate them. So sit down, and take a deep breath. You've got time. So take the time to be patient and humble and to do whatever work you're asked to do well. Any difference worth making in this world will be worth the work and worth the wait.

Not Just a Hobby

MOLLY SODA

In retrospect, school seems to be the easy part—you have a schedule, you know where you need to go and what you need to be doing.

Then you graduate.

I went to art school. I think a lot of art school graduates are taught to believe that art is not a career. Going to school to become an artist sort of seems like going to school to become a pop star. Your parents try to discourage you from pursuing an art degree—they want you to do something more "financially secure."

But it seems sort of silly that we're all told that we're going to fail as artists.

In many ways, that alone molds and shapes what we think about ourselves and what we think we can achieve.

I graduated from New York University with a degree in photography. I moved to Chicago because I thought it would be too scary to make it work in New York. Moving to Chicago was a welcome change of pace for me—but I was scared about entering the real world, as well as the art world, and failing. So I resigned myself to pursue art as a hobby.

I got a job working retail—somewhere that paid very little but that was relaxed enough that I could just coast by. I searched for art-related jobs—but super passively—I didn't know what I wanted to do, what the rest of my life was going to look like. Maybe I would become an elementary school art teacher; maybe I would work for a magazine.

Outside of work, my biggest resource postgraduation was the Internet. There lay all of my answers. I had spent my entire young adult / adult life up to this point sharing everything I did online. People saw it as superficial or shallow, but I saw it as absolutely necessary. I wouldn't have gotten through high school or college without it. I had the support, the love, the attention, and the care I always wanted online.

Eventually, opportunities began to come to me because I was constantly sharing my work and personal life online. I saw that people were paying attention, but I didn't see how to turn that attention into money or some sort of actual career. YouTube stars have ad revenue—but I was a digital artist. I put all of my work out on the Internet for free. It felt super discouraging. I had all of this attention, but I didn't understand what to do with it.

I continued to share and live my life the way I had been despite these frustrations. I continued to work my retail job— until one day, I got fired.

Getting fired was the best thing that could have ever happened to me. It forced me to take a look at my life, where I was and what I wanted. I had gotten comfortable riding this Internet art wave and hating my day-to-day work life. It forced me to look at why I was so focused on making a distinction between my URL and my IRL, and why I was so afraid of making my hobby my livelihood.

After losing that job, I decided that I was going to take the risk and become an artist full-time. I would work freelance, I would sell zines, I would do whatever it took to support myself as an artist—as long as I was happy and I was making work that I cared about, everything would fall into place. I knew it seemed like a sort of naïve and idealistic way of going about things, but I didn't know what else to do.

And it worked! I was so afraid of failing that I had never even tried. We are told we are going to fail as artists—that we need to prepare to fail in a sense. That's such a bummer. I'm glad I got out of that mode of thinking. Often the thing we call our hobby is what we are most passionate about, what we are capable of putting the most work into, and therefore the place where we have the potential to succeed.

Useful

→»«←

MARA WILSON

Graduating in the middle of the Great Recession meant being jobless. Graduating from college in the middle of the Great Recession with a theater degree meant being effectively useless.

To be fair, my degree came from a comprehensive interdisciplinary program; I just hadn't put enough work into it. Directing was too much pressure, I didn't have the eye to be a designer, and I didn't trust myself enough to commit to being a writer. I hadn't made the connections my friends had. But there had to be tons of job openings for dramaturgs and board operators!

There weren't.

Besides my "sordid past" as a mildly famous child actor and a few brief stints in retail and food service, the only real job I'd had was at a tutoring center. I spent the summer before college explaining first- and second-grade math to a group of Korean students. ("Did you know Koreans are allergic to Japanese?" asked a second-grade girl. It has to be the most innocent way I've ever heard anyone describe centuries of war and hatred.)

Despite my dramatic ambitions, I'd have to tutor again, because working with kids was one of the few things I knew how to do.

After contacting twenty organizations, one finally got back to me: a nonprofit that needed an after-school teacher at an underserved public elementary school.

"Just so you know," the supervisor told me right after she offered me the job, "half the teachers working here last year quit."

I quickly learned why. Rats ran up the cafeteria walls. Fifth graders fought so brutally the teachers called the police, and a third grader had to be talked out of throwing himself out a window. Second graders pointed out the drug dealers and undercover cops on the roofs across the street, and kindergartners sobbed in my arms because they missed their incarcerated parents. Learning disabilities went ignored. I worried when the first-grade teacher, Ms. Blanchard, who stamped correct homework papers with a personalized stamp that said, "YOUR A STAR!" quit not just in the middle of a semester but in the middle of a week.

It was a complex example of what's wrong with our public school system. The after-school program aspired to be a nurturing environment, but the supervisor who hired me went AWOL, leaving us without any plan for the rest of the year. Every day I looked around and wondered what I was doing there. I had no formal training in education, social work, or child development. All I had were my few months on the job and my recurring panic attacks. I felt useless.

You're here for the kids! I told myself. There were students I'd bonded with, like tiny pigtailed Gabriela, who drew beautiful pictures and never got in trouble. Or wiry Adrian, who said preternaturally witty things.

"How do you grow up to be an after-school teacher?" he asked one day, eyeing me skeptically.

I felt the need to defend myself to this small child. "I do other things, too! I . . . write stuff."

"Aw, you don't write!" he said. "All *you* ever write is who's on the Quiet Time list!"

He was funny and adorable but also had a knack for getting in trouble. Usually when a child got in trouble, it wasn't entirely his or her fault. When it was, we had to be careful how we told parents: sometimes they wouldn't believe their child could've ever done anything wrong. Other times, they were furious and quick to punish.

I thought about how my own father had reacted when I got in trouble. He had been strict, usually believing a teacher's word over mine; I was guilty until proven innocent. But he always allowed me to plead my case. I felt a rush of gratitude. I saw myself much more as my late mother's daughter. But I was also seeing my father's quiet and practical demeanor develop in myself. I was even starting to sound like him with the kids: "Keep an eye on the time." "What's the homework situation?"

He knew about my job, but he didn't know how hard it was. After one particularly difficult day, I called him.

"Dad, I don't think I can do this anymore." I told him everything. For twenty minutes, he listened. There was a long pause, but finally he spoke.

"Are you asking me for permission to quit?"

"I . . ." And I realized I was. I was becoming Ms. Blanchard.

"Because I'm not going to give that to you," he went on. "Don't quit. You took a job, you're helping those kids, and they have enough instability in their lives as it is."

"But I'm not good at it," I said. "I'm not a social worker. There's nothing I can do for them."

"You must be doing something, because they hired you. And it's your *job*. At least finish out the year. Don't quit in the middle."

And despite myself, I told the truth. "But I don't like it."

I felt ashamed. If there was one thing my father would not abide, it was entitlement. It was why my parents had made me share a room with my sister and shop for movie premiere dresses at Target. Being mildly famous wasn't going to go to my head. But there was only so much they could do. I'd been spoiled by circumstance. My first movie role had been my first movie audition, and I'd gone on to work regularly for the next six years. I'd understood that life would be unpredictable, and yet, when it came to a career, I'd never expected anything other than stability.

"Well, here's the thing," he said. "Most people *don't* like their jobs. Not all the time, anyway. They don't get all their happiness from what they do. They get it from their friends, their family . . . other places. Not everyone can define themselves by their job."

His tone was gentler than I'd expected. Maybe he knew I was already feeling ashamed. Hadn't I been seeing, firsthand, people living without all the opportunities I'd had?

"You know," he added, "the summer you were born, I was on strike. I couldn't get another job, I already had three kids to support, but you know what? I remember thinking, *I've never felt so alive.* And when it does come, when you get something closer to what you want—and it may not look like what you expected—you'll appreciate it more. Just do your job. You'll be glad you did."

For the next few months, I breathed through the panic attacks. I hugged the kindergartners and showed the third graders science experiments. I made sure there were other people, much more competent teachers, who could take my place. I did what my father suggested: I stuck it out until the end of the year.

It was not my life forever, but it was my job for that year. I wasn't useless. I was showing up, for my job and also for myself. Proving to myself that even though I was a bit lost, I was not going to quit.

Back-Pocket Feminism

→» «←

LORI ADELMAN

There was always going to be a particular kind of shit-eating humility that I'd face upon graduation. Modeling the "overachiever girl" archetype since elementary school, I'd clung desperately to the promise of meritocracy as a means of rescuing me from any unfair treatment I might experience as a young Black girl. At my school, people at least pretended they were neutral on race and gender, even if they actually held many of the stereotypes and double standards endemic to the broader society. An A was an A, and my task was straightforward if not easy: try to get them. If you're wondering how that worked out for me, well, how has stuff gone for most of the Black nerds you know? I was never going to graduate graciously into a world in which no one gave a shit about my standardized test scores or painstakingly spell-checked book reports, and isms ran free and unbridled, like wild horses.

While I may have been painfully earnest, I wasn't naïve. I understood intrinsically that the real world did not value rule-following perfectionist girls in quite the same manner as my felt scary to have my name associated with controversial top-ics on the Internet, and there was no hint of monetization to make things better at that time.

Eventually, I was hired at a small women's rights NGO. I continued blogging and in time came to not suck as a writer. I went on to take over site operations and be offered the oppor-tunity to work for numerous organizations helping to advance health and rights and fight gender-based injustice.

My experience of chaotic, tear-filled, postgrad panic wasn't unique. Many of us have it at different points in time. You can't always start out perfect, or really ever end up that way, either. It's a hard transition from girl-who-tries-too-hard to a proficient straight-A adult. Finding a place for myself as a professional feminist helped me embrace that fact, just not in the way I ini-tially thought it might. I feel privileged to work in a field I love and to enjoy some degree of success in that field. But I will al-ways have a special nostalgia for those months of humility. Feel-ing unarmed and raw helped me to home in on my real intentions and ambitions around racial and gender justice and realize why exactly I'd been drawn to feminism in the first place— not to be some perfect postgrad, but to finally be part of a community of people who understood.

Thongs Are a Bad Idea and Other Advice

LAURA WILLCOX

When I graduated from college, I was really excited to get a job. I was ready to be an adult who worked hard for the money and who then got to spend the money she made (Note: If you like affording restaurants or spending less than 60 percent of your income on rent, don't move to New York). (But do move here, it's an amazing place. So many restaurants!) More importantly, I wanted my first job to help me decide what I would *do* for the rest of my life because I really had no idea. I needed this job to define my future, my adulthood. No pressure!

So on a one hundred–degree day in July, I had a job interview with a filmmaker in New York who was looking for an assistant. He had me meet him at a Starbucks. Then when he showed up, he immediately suggested we go elsewhere because he actually "hates Starbucks, so corporate," so he took me to his "favorite Thai hole in the wall" so we could get bright orange Thai iced teas. Then I had my first real job interview in a nearby park in a sweltering heat wave. Not only did I spill bright orange Thai iced tea all over my pale green skirt but I later realized I had a thong-shaped sweat mark on my ass as well. Thongs are a bad idea, guys. I got the job anyway, which maybe should have been a red flag? But I was excited! Money! Freedom! A sense of purpose!

Before starting this job, I had these visions of my first job being awesome, working with creative types in New York, people who could be my mentors. Unfortunately, this boss was not that. He had made some decent documentaries at a young age, but now, twenty years later, he still had the ego of a hot-shot filmmaker without the reel to back it up. He was a terrible boss. His idea of running a small production company was talking people into doing lots of work for him for as little money as possible. He carried himself with the kind of unearned swagger and insufferable entitlement that only a white dude can have. He had clearly hoped to hire a young female assistant who would at the least revere him and at the most bang him or introduce him to her young, hot friends. Unfortunately for him, I was not that kind of assistant. It became clear pretty quickly that this man was not going to be the mentor I was looking for. And yet, despite how much I despised him, this was my boss, and I had this weird desire to earn his respect. I wanted him to take me seriously as a coworker and, you know, a human being. Anyway, we worked out of his tiny home office in his apartment. Needless to say, it wasn't a dream job, and it wasn't always super comfortable. But this was mid-recession, so I didn't feel like I had much of a choice but to stay. (Advice: Don't graduate in a recession.)

A year passed. One day the following summer, I had run downstairs to the bank to deposit some checks for my boss. I was waiting in line at the ATM when I suddenly had the urge to fart. I did a quick assessment of my surroundings: there were only a few other people in there, and besides, I could tell it was a small fart, so I let it rip.

And I shit myself. Wearing a sundress. On a ninety-five-degree day. In the ATM vestibule in my boss's building. It came out of nowhere. It was so shocking and cruel. I had no idea what to do. I couldn't go back upstairs to work; he'd smell me a mile away. The one saving grace was that I worked just thirteen blocks away from my apartment. So I clenched my butt and began the arduous walk home. Have you ever had one of those dreams where you're trying to run as fast as you can, but no matter how hard you try, your body continues to move in slow motion and you can't get anywhere? That's what walking thirteen blocks wearing a sundress and trying to not let liquid shit run down your leg feels like.

PSA time: I was wearing boy-cut underwear. They saved me. What if I had been wearing a thong? I can't even think about it. Don't ever wear thongs. Thongs are a bad idea.

So I finally got home, I jumped in the shower, I sobbed, I asked God why me, I burned my underwear. But I had to go back to work. I'd now been depositing checks for forty-five minutes. My dress was clean enough, so I kept that on. One less thing to explain. I went back to the "office," where my boss immediately asked where I had been. And I realized I had a choice: I could come up with some lie and save face and hope that he would someday value me as a coworker. Or I could give up on this dream of having a cool first boss that respects me and just proudly tell him the truth: I am a woman who shit her sundress, and I am officially *over* working for you, recession be damned!

So I took a deep breath, and I told him that my grandmother had been hit by a car. And I would need the next day off to pretend to go visit her in the hospital. Because sometimes making people pity you is the next best thing to respect. And for now, that was going to have to be good enough.

What to Look for in
a Workplace

NIA KING

When you are young, people assume you can work long hours for low wages and have no real adult responsibilities (like ailing parents or dependent children). Whether or not these assumptions are true, it's important to understand that as an entry-level worker, employers perceive you as an easily exploitable source of labor, especially when the job market is bad.

When you don't have a lot of work experience, it's hard to know what your time is worth and how to advocate for yourself. Some of these things you can only learn through experience, but there are a couple of good indicators regarding whether an organization or company will be a healthy work environment for you.

1. Do people stick around for a while? If your place of business has a high turnover rate, it usually becomes clear why pretty quickly after starting.

2. Is the pay decent? Before you agree to a salary or wage, do the math and see if you can actually live off that

amount. Budget not only for food, rent, utilities, transportation, and health insurance (if not provided) but also for student loans and any other monthly payments you need to make. Don't forget to deduct what you'll have to pay in taxes.

3. Are there benefits? Don't assume you are going to be young or healthy forever. Health insurance is really important, especially if you have health issues now or are likely to develop them due to family history or the working conditions at this new job.

4. Are there other people like you there? Are you going to be the only disabled person, the only person of color, or the only queer person at this job? How much energy are you willing to put into making your workplace a place where you feel safe and comfortable? Changing the culture of a workplace is unpaid and emotionally taxing labor you will be putting in on top of your paid job responsibilities.

5. If you can and it won't jeopardize your being offered the job, talk to people that work there that aren't the ones trying to recruit you. Use LinkedIn to find out who you know that knows someone that works there. Ask them what they really think. Do they seem happy? Frazzled? Burned out? Do they have hobbies? Hobbies imply that people still have time and energy after the workday is done.

6. Do you have anything in common with your coworkers outside of what drew you to the job? You don't have

to be BFF with everyone you work with, but if you could see yourself hanging out with them outside of work, you will probably last longer there.

7. Do the people seem nice? This might seem silly, but some bosses give off strong sadist vibes even before they hire you. Trust your gut.

Despite your best efforts to identify red flags, you might find yourself working at a place where you are undervalued, not given the tools or guidance you need to succeed, or made to feel like you are not good at what you do. As a young person, a woman, a queer person, a person of color, a disabled person, and so on, people may try to make you out to be uppity or like you should be grateful just to have a job. This can be really crazy-making.

Try your best, but when your best isn't good enough, stop assuming that the problem is you. Some jobs are not going to be the right fit, and sometimes you are not going to realize they are not the right fit until you are six months, twelve months, or eighteen months deep. It's unfortunate, but not unfixable.

If there's nothing keeping you there, leave. If fear of poverty is keeping you there, figure what you can do to network with people that have the kinds of jobs you *actually* want while you are still employed. Ideally, you want to find a new better job before leaving your old one.

Sometimes you can't quit because you're in too much debt or because people depend on you financially. If you are chained to a nightmare job, I'm sorry. Hopefully, you have a meaning-ful life outside of work that makes it bearable and worthwhile. If not, try to identify what you might be able to do to develop one.

If you do end up quitting, remember that *quitting isn't failing*. When a relationship isn't working, eventually the healthiest thing you can do is get out of it. The same is true with jobs. Not being able to make it work at one place doesn't mean you are not cut out for the real world or the job market; it just means you are not cut out for that particular job.

I left my last nonprofit job feeling totally worthless. I was told by my boss that coworkers cringed when I walked in a room. I was told by coworkers that if I really cared about the organization's mission, I would be happy to scrub the toilets. I was told this is what the real world was like, and I needed to learn how to deal with it, because things wouldn't be better anywhere else. None of these things were true.

It took me a while after leaving the job to realize I wasn't the problem and to redevelop my self-esteem. I had to figure out what I was good at, what I liked doing, and what gave me life. In the years since I left that job, I started the podcast *We Want the Airwaves*, published the book *Queer & Trans Artists of Color*, and toured the United States and Canada with two different queer people of color arts organizations. I know now that I am not worthless, but for a long time I blamed myself for not being able to make it work at my old job and not being grateful just to be employed.

Today I have a job where I am evaluated based on my performance, not on my personality. My current job pays my bills and still leaves time for making art. My wages are lower than at my nonprofit job, and I don't have benefits, but I'm getting by.

Bad jobs teach you a lot about yourself, like what's really important to you and what you can do without. They also help you learn how to identify the red flags of an unhealthy work environment much better for the future.

Part of your twenties is going to be spent doing things you are bad at and don't like so that you can figure out what you are good at and do like. Failure is inevitable, but it's how you learn, not how the story ends.

Not for Me

>> <<

WHITNEY MIXTER

In college, you could have found me sitting at my desk with copious amounts of coffee running through my system, clacking away at a keyboard as the sun rose. I'd no doubt be surrounded by a plethora of makeshift ashtrays, trying desperately to get the creative world living inside my head out on paper, my fingers just not typing fast enough. Sounds like the tortured author, right?

Well, that was me, all right. But not so much the next Hunter S. Thompson and more just another overwhelmed student on day three of no sleep. Double major, two full-time jobs, an internship at the biggest LGBT law firm in the world. I was the definition of busy. It was a love-hate relationship. On one hand, I was entrenched in the constant rush of the go-go-go mentality, sure that I was on track to solve world peace one term paper and folded Urban Outfitters sweater at a time, while on the other hand I was too exhausted to notice any better.

And then, I graduated!

I now had a cum laude bachelor's degree in both political

science and women's studies and, although impressive on paper, I knew my next step wasn't exactly the Oval Office. After the diploma was passed and the tassel was turned, I realized I had no idea what came next. There was no class that had prepared me for actual "this is your future—make something of it" real life! I went from being so busy doing busywork that when it all came to a halt I had a hard time creating my own game plan for success.

I needed a plan. Law school sounded like the next reasonable decision, and I knew it would give me another chance to bide time before starting "real life," so I picked up the books and began my LSAT prep.

The LSATs aren't exactly something you take for fun. I spent hours upon hours training my brain to function in a way that it hadn't before, learning terminology and analytical thinking techniques out the wha-zoo-tee, and still subconsciously the little inner me was screaming, "*Why are you doing this?*"

Needless to say, I took the test. But as I walked out of the exam auditorium, looking around at all of those other J.D. potentials, pale from their uncertain results, I realized this was their life, not mine. They knew this was what they wanted to do with a definitiveness that I did not have. I couldn't imagine another four years of school, let alone another $100,000 more in debt and a career as, of all things, a lawyer!

But then, what *did* I want? I knew I wanted to make a difference. I knew I wanted to use my voice to reach people. And I knew I wanted to make them laugh. That may sound like a career in law to some, but I now know that wasn't what it meant for me.

At first it seemed like it was back to the drawing board, but this academic close call ended up being my saving grace. I started taking my first steps toward redefining what busy meant for me and creating a life that I would love.

For the first time, my life wasn't dictated by what I thought I was supposed to do but instead by what I wanted to do. This flexibility exposed a new side of myself, one less defined by lists and quantitative results and instead focused on creativity and entrepreneurship. I moved from the East Coast to LA with my dogs and a job opportunity joining my best friend in a special effects makeup endeavor for the military. Talk about a 180.

It was the concept of letting go and actually not having a plan for once that got me cast on a little show called *The Real L Word* on Showtime almost immediately following my move to Los Angeles. Now let me get something straight: I'm in no way saying to give up your academia for dreams of grandeur in Hollywood. What I am saying is be open, trust your journey, and show up in life.

When I left the LSATs that day, I made up my mind to pursue what I truly wanted and to blaze my own path to get it. I wanted to know and be known. And what did this reevaluation and proaction lead to? I spent the next four years of my life participating in two different docuseries while creating a lucrative event business and guest spotting on various politically focused webcasts. I've learned more about myself and have grown tremendously from the bare-all approach I took in the production of *The Real L Word*, however scary and exposing it may have been at times. I've been able to use my notoriety as a platform for causes dear to me, such as animal welfare and women's and LGBT rights.

Above all, I have created my own *busy*, and in doing so, I

have achieved all of the core things I wanted in life, all while having a blast doing it. A wise man by the name of Dr. Seuss once wrote, "*You have brains in your head. You have feet in your shoes. You can steer yourself any direction you choose.*"

Doing the Dishes

EMILY GOULD

In 2003, during my final year of college, I was one of a large team of unpaid interns at a small but nationally distributed feminist magazine. Our duties included washing the editor in chief's dishes and taking out the garbage. We also filled subscriptions manually, by transcribing handwritten forms into a creaky computer system. The open-plan office had once been the art director's apartment, and the intern-to-employee ratio was something like four to one; the place basically ran on unpaid labor. No one had thought to protest unpaid internships yet. I mean, we protested privately to each other as we smoked cigarettes downstairs while taking out the garbage, but there was no organized labor movement decrying unpaid internships for being unfair to people who can't afford to work for free the way there is now.

In retrospect, it seems ridiculous to me that I tolerated being used as, essentially, an unpaid janitor, but at first I thought the job's perks outweighed its downside. I got bylines in the magazine! (Which meant, of course, that I was also writing for free.) I also got to take home a lot of sparkly makeup that I never used, and occasionally we interns would get to take the CDs that the magazine received for review to the used CD store, sell them, then lie about how much money we'd received and use our ill-gotten gains to buy ourselves cigarettes. (This was back when people still bought both CDs and cigarettes.)

Even after it became clear to me that a folder of clips of my two hundred–word makeup and music reviews wasn't going to catch the eye of the editors of *The New Yorker*, I stayed in this mostly thankless role because I was terrified of what was going to happen to me after I graduated that winter, and I had convinced myself that, of all the many interns, I would be the one chosen to become one of the tiny magazine's employees.

Now, I have made a living for most of the past decade by writing, and one of the things I get kudos for on a regular basis is my eye for detail. And it's true: I have a great eye for detail! But, then as now, I sometimes have a problem seeing the big picture. The big picture, in this case, was that this magazine was never in a million billion years going to hire me. In fact, as I outstayed my welcome there by a semester—I basically just refused to stop showing up after the semester was over—I made myself more and more unpopular. I couldn't hide my resentment about doing the dishes, and my stank attitude disendeared me to the editor in chief. I should have quit, but instead I redoubled my commitment, volunteering for more work even as I complained relentlessly every time I thought my bosses weren't listening. Meanwhile, a member of the new crop of interns was getting her pitches approved and going out drinking with the editorial assistant we interns all revered and feared. She would, of course, be the one who ended up getting hired.

Eventually, the editor in chief took me to Starbucks and gently informed me that I should move on in order to give someone else the opportunity that I'd had. I was so naïve at the time that I didn't realize I was being fired; I am almost certain I kept showing up at the office for days (weeks? months?) after this happened.

Sometimes I think about how different my life trajectory would have been if I'd been able to conceal my innate jerkiness well enough to stay on the magazine's good side and had gotten that job I thought I so desperately wanted. My career hasn't exactly been a string of unmitigated successes, but on the other hand, I've done what I wanted to do. The intern who got hired, last I checked, was still working at that magazine. I don't think they still make her wash the dishes, but you never know.

High Fives for Trying

→*←

ERIC ANTHONY GLOVER

I got fired from my first real job out of college. Turned out being madly in love with my position wasn't the same as being ready for it, and despite my preference for lessons learned the easy way, I needed to know the difference.

But even as I began to move on, I was afraid I'd lost something arguably more precious than the job: that gleeful, unconscious filter through which I'd seen new adulthood, making each success *meant to be* and each setback speed-bump-bearable, part of my path, for my own good, and behind me soon. The real world suddenly came into focus as a shifting, sharp-edged thing that owed me nothing and, more hauntingly, offered no high fives for trying.

That concept began to curdle in the summer of the same year, by which time my unemployment had overstayed its welcome and my A/C-less apartment felt like a reckoning of life choices. To boot, an online campaign I was running—designed to raise awareness about disability underrepresentation in comics—had reached a middling middle phase. Although I'd managed to gain some publicity at first, I was running out of places to find support, a promising call I'd had with a disability nonprofit had proven fruitless, and I was struggling to reach celebrities who might help. That even included writer-director Kevin Smith, a self-professed comics geek who should have been an easy sell, given how often he talked superheroes on his weekly podcasts. I'd barraged him with tweets and e-mailed his website, but his silence felt somehow expected. And maybe, more realistically, *inevitable*.

The summer, like everything else, was starting to sting.

Especially on the day I finally purchased an air conditioner with my girlfriend. It was a hulking, cumbersome contraption—requiring in setup a stubbornly rigid plastic tube, a tray receptacle for watery runoff, and a patience known only to Christ. The process had exhausted us by hour one, and by hour three, our grips on sanity were feeling sweatier. Daylight eventually died out, and the dream of cooler air was transforming into something that felt dangerously quixotic.

A fly had also gotten into our living room, which wasn't especially out of the ordinary—but it felt pointedly, unacceptably unfair at the time. My girlfriend watched as I willfully gave into a crazed, irrational fixation with killing it, hoping that swatting at where it landed—a living room windowpane—would lead to a short-term, desperately needed, just-this-once sensation of conquest. Instead, I broke the glass and bloodied my hand.

Given all that, I'm not sure why, in retrospect, we chose to listen to a Kevin Smith podcast to pass the time. Logic dictated his voice would only remind me of how poorly things had gone—that night, that summer, that year—and it would've been reasonable to assume hearing him talk about comics would just twist the knife.

But not long into his program, he began to discuss my campaign by name. He read its mission statement aloud to his followers. He discussed what he agreed with and disagreed with about my position—but overall presented my cause and concerns fairly.

As a result of his help, the followers on my campaign's Facebook page increased. I went on to use the podcast to push my initiative further—with more legitimacy than I'd been able to muster up on my own. (Several months later, my girlfriend and I were even able to thank Smith for his help in person.)

Of course, as much as I was indebted to Smith for the sake of the campaign, I was also grateful for the general reminder that "shit show" might not always be life's default setting. The hard work of pushing myself anyway—and pushing myself *better*—remained, to be sure. I continue that work to this day.

I got that damn air conditioner working eventually. And the real world, at least that night, didn't seem so scarce on high fives anymore. Even if this one had left my hand a little bloody.

PART TWO

»«

Home and Belonging

Locked Out

BIJAN STEPHEN

I slept outside on my first night in New York City. This was late August or early September, about three years ago, and I lived in Greenpoint then. I'd picked up my keys from the realtor—who bade me good-bye with a fun and flirty "Congratulations!"—and that night I went with a friend to some forgettable bars in Alphabet City. We drank; we fought. Instead of staying with her, the original plan, I said *fuck it* and headed back to my new apartment, with her air mattress (which she'd lent me earlier) in tow. Looking back now, I'm not exactly sure what month it was. I know it was late summer, though, because when the heat rose from the asphalt that night it wasn't harsh.

I recently finished *Inferno (A Poet's Novel)*, Eileen Myles's disorienting novel-memoir on discovering poetry, discovering sex, discovering love, coming out, and learning how to live in New York. The prose is glancing and affectless. "That that could be the stuff of novels, a world so much like the world I now inhabited," she writes, "that my own newness could be gone, a myth." I think I understand what Myles is talking about, if only because I live there now.

It wasn't always that way. I grew up in Tyler, Texas, a small town in the eastern part of the state. It was suburban and Southern, which is a deadly combination: racist, religious, *and* boring. I'm still learning how to write about it, though I lived there for over a decade. Leaving felt like waking up after having been deeply asleep; when your eyes are closed, you're not dead, not quite, but that's the closest most of us come to the event before it takes us.

I have an inveterate habit of journaling. I do this to convince myself that what happens to me is real. It's a habit that's come, I think, from being very young in Texas; casual racism has a funny way of gaslighting you, making you wonder if the world—as Eileen sees it, as I see it, as you see it—really is the way people say it is. Because what if reality's tilted a few degrees further than you thought it was? How would you know, if you didn't write anything down?

I will say, however, that I am extremely bad at keeping a journal. The reason I stay at it—maybe this time will be different!—is the reason I fail: I'm not yet sure what's worth recording. (In the meantime, I suppose Google keeps a record of all of my chats.) If *Inferno* is any guide, Eileen writes poetry for the same reason. I'm paraphrasing her idea here, but she *pulls* the right words from her experiences. Right out of thin air. They're already there—you only have to array them *just so*. The New York poets and rappers seem to understand this. Take, for example, my favorite Frank O'Hara poem, "St. Paul and All That." "Totally abashed and smiling / I walk in / sit down and / face the frigidaire," he begins; the poem slouches forward in the same register, uncertain and perhaps a little yielding. "[S]uch little things have to be established in the morning / after the big things of night," O'Hara writes a bit farther down, referring to the impossibility of understanding time, knowing when exactly you are.

Years before I knew the poem, I tried the same thing. I was in college then, my first real home, and I think it was a snowy October. On the fridge in a friend's room, there were rearrangeable magnetic words. We wrote haiku:

1. White winter storm heaves
You trudge as wind blows above
Avoid death by fluff

2. Recall rainwater
A lazy petal sleeps bare
Smooth peach symphony

3. I have a spring crush
My sweet chocolate boyfriend
I am enormous

But it's not so important. I will elide that part of me, except to say: First, that I studied biology, and it has left me with an enduring impulse to know the ways things work. Second, I realized then I'd be trying to understand ecosystems for the rest of my life.

→«

A biological fact I like: We all live in the past, because there are millisecond delays in experience; the electrical impulses that travel through your neural architecture are quick, but not fast enough to deliver reality as it happens. The brain weaves the signals together, which creates the illusion that the movie inside your head is continuous. Your brain decides what is and what isn't important, what to keep for later and what to immediately discard.

I was so aware of that, my first year in New York. I remember the long walks I'd take in the mornings and sometimes drunk at night, when the world holds its breath because the guard is changing. I kept a record of those trips. Sometimes I texted friends my observations; when I was alone at night, feeling the liquor slosh around, I wrote them down.

There is a kind of power in this, I think. Because when you write things down, you have a little control over how they happen; you can sometimes even control how you feel. Here, I could tell you what I think about using that power. But I'd rather tell you the end of the story I started before.

That night in Greenpoint, the moon was full. I tried my new door with the keys I'd been given; they didn't work. My phone had been stolen the week before, and my work phone was dead. A drunk man on the corner pointed me to the dive bar I'd visit many times over the years. I walked inside. *Whiskey double, neat, please*, I said, feeling very much like a character in a student film. The people there took pity on me; at 4:30 A.M., they passed around some weed, and suddenly you could smoke cigarettes inside.

I walked back to my apartment building around 6:00 A.M., when the black sky was just beginning to shade into the deep blue it takes on before it shatters into pink. I lay on my back on my stoop; it was quiet, and I was alone, waiting for the world to exhale.

That bar closed down recently, so I'm not a regular anymore. My newness isn't gone, but it also isn't a myth. I guess what I'm trying to say is simple: New York, I think, has always felt like home.

Moving Back Is Not
a Step Back

➤➤⬅

NISHA BHAT

Baby steps are the key to life after graduation. Maybe you've just graduated and are moving back with your parents. Perhaps you're wondering if that's the right move. Possibly, you feel like it's a step back, a sign that you're not a "real" adult after all. If any of that rings true for you, don't you worry. I felt that as well, even though I knew it was common for recent grads to move back home after college. It is a tremendous effort to accept a loss of freedom and independence, to a considerable extent, even though it's incredibly commendable that you've earned a degree and are ready to start a new, exciting era in your life. You're not a failure for returning to your hometown and home-cooked food. This is true even if you don't have a job yet; in fact, it's especially true if you don't have a job yet.

Let me just say that again: You're not a failure. You're not a failure for not having a job immediately after graduating, or for coming back home for a bit, or for taking a break after earning your degree.

Having a high-paying, amazing job upon graduation is a dream for many—a very sexy dream. It's also not the norm. It takes time to apply for positions. It takes time to hone your professional skills, such as perfecting your résumé, learning how to tweak cover letters for every position, and working on your LinkedIn profile. You may be thinking, *Yeah, whatever. I know my résumé is kick-ass, and I can churn out cover letters in my sleep.* I congratulate you and your extraordinary slumbering cerebral cortex. Even so, I encourage you to continuously work on your professional persona, because you never know when a recruiter will suddenly e-mail you with a job opportunity. I know, because it happened to me. I'll get to that in a bit.

After graduating, there was a definite moment in which I finally accepted that I was on the right track to postgrad life, even if I hadn't quite believed it before. My family and I traveled to India in June to visit my relatives and complete a sort of coming-of-age ceremony for my brother. The weeks between graduating and leaving for India were a strange mix of rampant graduation celebration (highly recommended) and meticulously preparing luggage, verifying tickets, and choosing the proper vegetarian airplane meals for the trip (not quite as highly recommended, or fun). Every two or three years since I was six months old, I have visited my extended family in India, yet once I landed and finally breathed in the humid air in my grandparents' house, I knew that this trip was different. I suppose now I know that's because I wasn't the same.

One day, we climbed into my grandparents' car and rumbled along to visit my dad's cousin and his wife. While munching on some savory snacks, I tuned in to the conversation around me. The topic of discussion was the college experience, degrees, and jobs. The entire concept of success in India hinges on entrance exams and rankings more than it does in the United States, and doing a double major in two different fields, as I had done, is uncommon, sometimes not even possible. When my dad's cousin heard that I had just gotten my bachelor of science in neuroscience and economics with a minor in chemistry, he said to me, "You are very lucky to have earned such a wonderful degree. Everyone is so proud of you."

I blinked slowly as his words sank into my brain. *Wow, I guess that's really true*, I remember thinking vaguely. *It is pretty awesome to have finally earned it, and I'm so lucky.* The acknowledgment may sound trivial now, but at the time I felt like I hadn't done enough because I still hadn't been able to secure a job, and being in India where I was unable to continue applying did not assuage my fears. It's really the small moments that become significant in life.

After returning from India (and getting over the horrible jet lag), I was once more back home postgraduation, almost as though nothing had changed. It took quite some time before an opportunity opened up. As I said earlier, you really never know when a recruiter will e-mail you out of the blue. I opened up LinkedIn one day, and there appeared a message from a company I'd never heard of. One thing led to another, and now I have a job! I am employed, but I still live at home. I had always thought that I would return home for a little bit and then secure a job in some other city and move into my own apartment before I ever started a career. Earlier, I even seriously considered going abroad to teach English right after graduating in May. Plans change and so do people, and it is best to keep that in mind as you continue forward, whether it is finishing your degree or moving back home after earning it.

→←

Moving back is not a step back. Just keep working on yourself, go with the flow, enjoy living at home again, and know that you'll kick-start a wonderful career soon enough.

One-Way Ticket to Paris

⇥⇤

SHANNON KEATING

Nine months after graduating from college, I bought a one-way ticket to Paris.

I'd spent the time since graduation working as an admissions counselor for my school, interviewing sweaty-palmed teenagers about their fledgling collegiate hopes and dreams. I drove rental cars to high schools throughout the Northeast, giving earnest presentations about how great my college experience had been, swallowing my jealousy that for all the kids I spoke to, the best was still ahead of them.

It was a pretty weird time. Plenty of my friends were still students, so I sat in the library scoring my applications while everyone else buzzed around me, high on chocolate-covered espresso beans, complaining about this class or that paper. I was grateful to spend time with them, especially since I'd graduated a year early, but I was caught in social limbo: not quite a grown-up, not quite a college kid. When I'd go to the campus bar, seniors slopping their beers asked me if I felt weird spending so much time around students—as if I were a crusty, old, out-of-touch *adult* adult and not a fellow twenty-two-year-old who'd been going to dumb themed parties with them all since freshman year.

When the Connecticut winter limped its way into a drizzly gray spring, I decided it was time to get the hell out of there.

My cost of living had been low—I rented a modest apartment on campus, and my rugby teammates smuggled me into the dining hall for team dinners whenever they could. I'd saved up enough of my salary to last me a few employment-free months. After applying to volunteer with an international film festival in Paris, I sprung for a plane ticket. My friends threw me a surprise going-away party the day before my flight; I got drunk on a two-liter bottle of merlot and cried myself to sleep on my best friend's bed.

Graduation all those months ago finally felt real. I was leaving.

I didn't know anyone in France. I didn't speak French. Already, I forget the reasons I chose to go for that particular film festival in that particular city. All I'd known was that sometime very soon, I'd get going on a legit career path, and opportunities to fly to a foreign country more or less on a whim would seriously dwindle. My student loan payments had just kicked in; I couldn't hide from them forever. But I could throw some savings their way and hide, for a time, in Paris.

When I landed, armed with nothing but one of those obnoxiously large hiker's backpacks stuffed with black T-shirts, I found Paris exploding in early spring bloom. My bus dumped me unceremoniously in a quiet corner of the city, and I decided to totter on foot all the way to the Airbnb I'd booked. My back threatened to crack in half a couple of miles in, but I soldiered on, buoyed by the stupid levels of beauty in which I'd found myself steeped.

>«

My Airbnb was in Montmartre, the 18th arrondissement, nestled on a hill behind the Sacré-Cœur in the northernmost pocket of Paris. Twisting little cobblestone streets hoisted themselves up, and up, and up, lined by overflowing fish markets pungent with brine; boulangeries radiating the thick, yeasty heat of freshly baked bread; tiny crowded cafés; wine shops the size of broom closets; fromageries stacked to the ceiling with hulking rounds of cheese and jars of jams that twinkled in the afternoon sun. I wanted to stop everywhere, but my backpack took up as much room as another two humans—and I realized that I'd have plenty of time to explore later, on my own unencumbered time, the whole city spread out like a promise at my feet.

I found my rental on a steeply inclined street, awash in the greens and whites of birch trees flanking the sidewalk. The owner met me there, walked me up six flights of spiral stairs, wished me well, gave me the heavy brass key. My apartment was a *chambre de bonne*—an old maid's chamber, the relic of bygone days in many creaky old buildings in Paris. I had a twin bed tucked under a slanted ceiling, my one window a skylight. I had a square yard of linoleum under a foldout kitchen table. I had a teeny, tiny kitchen sink with a hot plate across from a teeny, tiny shower. All one room. The toilet was out in the hallway.

It was ridiculous. I loved it very much.

Adjusting to life in Paris was preposterously effortless. My internship at the film festival proved to be zany and intimate, a small ragtag team of twentysomething film lovers from all over the world packed into a corner office in the bustling 11th arrondissement. Many were students who stopped by to help out when they got out of class; a few, like me, were interning full-time. I filled my days reading scripts, watching shorts, and brainstorming silly promotional videos to film around the city. We took breaks often, my coworkers-turned-friends and I, in typical French fashion: long indulgent lunches, all of us toting warm, fresh sandwiches of dried meat and jams to Place de la République or Canal Saint-Martin where we'd eat and laze in the sun; coffee breaks every hour, on the hour, espressos from the café across the street and hand-rolled cigarettes beneath the overhang when it rained.

My friends were Greek, Italian, Russian, French. We talked endlessly about cinema and politics, exploring the uncharted territory of our very different homelands. I'd take the Metro home, stop for a baguette, and eat half of it while walking back to my itty-bitty apartment, which always felt like returning to an old friend. In the evenings, I lay in bed reading, occasionally forcing my body awkwardly up through my skylight to look around the pink-tinged city quieting with nightfall: the many pale buildings fringed with pops of colorful shutters, flower baskets stirring sleepily in their windows. And every morning, I woke to soft, gray daylight, feeling quietly content—the most consistent contentment, day after day, I've ever felt. Then or since.

Of course, this Paris—my Paris—wasn't really *real*. For the only time in my life, I didn't have to worry about money—I'd told myself that this was my postgrad moment of reckless abandon, and I could spend all the cash I'd painstakingly saved without guilt. I didn't give a shit about what I'd do whenever I went home to the States. On the weekends, I wrote in my journal in elegantly manicured gardens—a different garden every day—eating *pain au chocolats* that crumbed in my lap. I went on dates with women from a bunch of different countries, kissed them over wine outside of cafés beneath the heat lamps. And I walked, and walked, and walked: down the Seine at twilight; through farmers' markets heaped with fruit and cheese; on an elevated railway-turned-park spilling over with roses. Always listening to music, always smoking a cigarette (something I'd have to quit when I left Paris—but that, like all other vices I'd acquired, could wait), always feeling like I was exactly where I was supposed to be.

Before I moved back to the United States, where I started working in media and got swirled into the everyday banalities of rent and laundry, I traveled throughout France and Spain and Ireland. I met a bunch of pretty awesome people—but it was all the time I spent alone, for hours on end in strange and mystical places, that I savored (and still savor) the most.

My time in Paris, and throughout Europe, was a big old cliché: beautiful, fleeting, precious. I don't regret a single cent I spent on those experiences, which I carry around with me every day. But now as I spend more and more time in the so-called real world, in the hustle, paying my loans and doing my dishes, I've been starting to worry that I will always measure my life—which, don't get me wrong, is a really, really good life—against the absolutely bonkers magic life I lived for a few months in my favorite city in the world.

Last month, I went back to Paris for the first time since leaving two years ago. I was on a weeklong business trip, visiting one of my company's outer offices. During the day, I plucked away at my computer, surrounded by the quick, ebullient French of my coworkers, feeling slightly lonely. (Working in the English-speaking film festival office my first time in Paris, I realized, had been an unprecedented gift.) At night, I stole away to various pockets of the city, revisiting the places and the people I loved. One evening, over drinks with a friend at a crowded café, she asked me how it felt to be back. "Does it feel different?"

And it did. When I'd first arrived on that trip, staying in a more commercial part of the city instead of my beloved Montmartre, I'd been slightly crestfallen to realize that, happy as I was to relive certain aspects of those few short, perfect months, the enchantment had faded somehow. But fading enchantment was actually a pretty great outcome, weird as that may sound: I finally figured out that there hadn't been some perfect, alternative life carrying on without me in Paris all this time. Those months had been a product of timing, just as much as a product of place. Slathering my twentieth bread chunk of the night with soft cheese, I told my friend that yes, it was different this time—different enough that, a few days later, packing up to leave and go home felt right. It even felt good. Like there was a chance the best might still be yet to come.

Walking Up the Hill

→≪

LANE MOORE

Paul said he remembered me from the job interview. I was crouched in a ball with my arms around my legs like I was holding a bag of oranges I didn't want to share. It was easily my fiftieth interview in weeks, having applied anywhere that would give me money to come in every day and do *something*. I'd already "auditioned" for a lot of other jobs, which involved me working full-day shifts and them not paying me at the end, saying I wasn't quite right for it and they'd let me know. I didn't realize at the time that they were just getting free labor. This is one of many things I did not know when I walked up the steep, impossible hill every day to the apartment I lived in with a man who said he wasn't sure what his name was. It at no point occurred to me that he was crazy.

I'm not sure what I thought adulthood was. If you asked me to describe what it felt like, I would've said: alone, without much hope that things will get better. I'd escaped from all of the things I hated back home, except for the feeling that I would continue to push boulders up that hill every day and dodge the street harassment that followed me up its incline while I carried home the small pile of vegetables I ate nightly in the dark until it killed me.

This job interview was a group interview, where all we talked about was music. What our favorite artists were, favorite albums, favorite songs. This I could do. I could be quietly funny and wait-what-did-she-just-say smart. Paul followed me home. Halfway through the walk home, he pushed me in a shopping cart so we could get back to my place faster. My feet were tired anyway, so I didn't mind. High school had happened in what felt simultaneously like one and also forty-five years ago. I was an adult now. No grown-ups, no supervision, no one to come get me. Not that there had been before, but now I was a girl in a city like thousands before and after me. Walking up a hill and down it, standing around, making a little bit of money and wondering if this was it. If this is all it was. Just taking what you've been given and being grateful you made it out of your hometown.

Paul and I became friends. I'd visit him in his apartment, a one-room shithole with two Murphy beds that never had fitted sheets on them; just bare mattresses stained with sweat from him and other twenty-year-old boys who came out to LA to make it as . . . whatever. It all seemed like a depressing sleep-away camp or a boarding school where parents who don't have any money send children they hate. Just waiting around for someone to come and give us money or jobs, to see that we were talented, that we Had It. Constantly looking at every single man who called me a young Audrey Hepburn with the hope that he would be the one to break my career open and save me from walking up that hill.

Everyone told me this was where I needed to be. Why work at some crappy little store in your hometown when you could work at a crappy little store *and* audition for movies? Where you can drink nothing but tea to keep your hands warm and gently fold the clothes you were wearing when you told the boy you thought you'd marry that you had other things to do right now. Things like walking up that hill and waiting to be discovered. Things like calling your friends and telling them you'd "made it" just by being there. And yeah. It was going great.

Paper Maps

KRISTIN RUSSO

I moved to New York City when I was nineteen. I'm not sure that there's ever been a place that sparkled and shone quite as much as NYC did for me that year, teeming with tangles of dirty streets, angry, honking cabs, and an endless array of scuttling rodents. I'd dreamed of this for years. Finally, it was all mine.

When I first arrived, I rented a tiny room in a hostel on the Upper West Side. My room had everything I needed: a twin bed, a desk, a mini-fridge, a heating pipe (which would burst a few weeks after I moved in, soaking all of my belongings and my brand-new forty-pound laptop), a sink, and a closet with three hangers. I shared a bathroom and a kitchen with five strangers who lived in my hallway.

At the time, I was finishing up my undergraduate degree in theater at Marymount Manhattan College. Marymount was on East Seventy-First Street, and my hostel was on West Ninety-Fourth Street. I studied the subway map (a paper map! I actually had a paper subway map!) to determine the best route between my new home and my new school. If I took the 2 train south to Times Square, I could transfer to the S train that would shuttle me across to Grand Central Station. Once there, I could transfer to the 4 train, one stop up to Fifty-Ninth Street and *then* transfer *one more time* to the 6 train to Sixty-Eighth. Boom. Four trains, no problem. This was city life. Yes!

I took those four trains twice a day. Not to brag, but I also learned how to get down to the NYU dorms at the South Street Seaport, where my then-girlfriend lived. (She was my very first girlfriend, and she was a *great* girlfriend. She let me smoke her cigarettes, wear her clothes, and borrow her wonderful CD mixes for my Discman-accompanied commutes.) One fateful day, I left her dorm and headed to catch the 4 train (another added bonus of staying at her place was that it only required two trains). I was wearing my favorite pair of overalls, which incidentally belonged to her and had legs that were wide enough to fit around my whole body. As I pushed through the subway trestle, I saw my train pull into the station. It had apparently only taken me three months of city living to begin to have the mind of a New Yorker, because my first instinct was to run as fast as I could to catch that train. And so, I ran.

And then, I fell.

Well . . . I *almost* fell. Truthfully, it would have been much better had I just fallen. Instead, my right foot caught in the wide swath of denim that surrounded it, and as I descended, I caught myself on the side of my left foot . . . and broke it.

Three months into moving to NYC, in the freezing November cold, I broke my goddamn foot.

I didn't immediately know I'd broken it, but I did know that I was in a massive amount of pain. Not too much pain, however, to continue my now one-legged sprint to catch that train. And I did! I caught the train! No one cheered for me, but now that I understand the spirit of NYC a bit better, I'm certain they were all cheering on the inside. Once on the train and in the wake of this very real, very extreme pain, I lost awareness of what was and wasn't acceptable train behavior. I dropped my bags in the middle of the train floor, I took off my giant winter coat, dropped it next to my bags, and I stared at my foot. That's all I did. I just stared at my foot, sweating with pain, brow furrowed, with my belongings all around me on the subway floor. I stared at it all the way to Forty-Second Street, scooped up my things, and hobbled across the plat-form to transfer to the 6 train, dropped them once more on the subway floor, stared at my foot until we got to Sixty-Eighth Street, and then somehow walked, on my freshly broken foot, to my acting class. It took me almost thirty minutes to walk three street blocks and one avenue. For reference, that's less than half a mile.

As you might expect, upon my arrival to class, my professor immediately told me to go to the walk-in clinic down the street. After x-rays, I was given a blue canvas boot and a pair of crutches, and I hobbled my way to an indulgent taxi ride back to my hostel.

In case you are unfamiliar with NYC winters, I will let you know that they are cold, they are icy, they are dirty, and they are entirely unforgiving—and all that with two working feet. I want to also remind you that my commute, up until this point, included about eight trains per day, and each of those came with ample walking and many stairs. I couldn't get up and down stairs much at all, and certainly not when they were cov-ered in icy slush. Suddenly, canvas boot and all, I couldn't get anywhere.

Until, that is, I revisited my subway map and learned that

NYC, in addition to its sprawling subway system, also has *buses*. *Who. Knew.* I learned (via my paper map) that just a few steps from my door was a crosstown bus that, on the regular, traveled *right through Central Park to the east side.* I'd been taking four trains this whole time when I could have taken *just one bus?* This was the first moment where the NYC I thought I knew laughed directly in my face before playfully tousling my hair. You see, NYC isn't shy about breaking a person, bones and all, in a gesture of the warmest welcome.

I've now been in this city for fifteen years. I know almost every subway line and bus route that exists in nearly every borough. I traverse it with the same ease that I brush my teeth or climb into my bed. That moment, fifteen years ago in lower Manhattan, was the first of many moments (they really never stop) where I was forced to readjust, recalibrate, and further question the city, and world, around me. I had many other pivotal moments in those first few years—some with only a handful of subway passengers as my witness, and others where the whole world watched my city in confusion and wonder.

We all, inevitably, break our metaphoric (or in my case, literal) feet. Am I glad that I broke my foot? Not really. Am I glad that it made me recalibrate, readjust, and continue to question? You'd better believe I am. I needed to learn, just as we all do, that there is always more than one route on that paper map.

Getting Things Going

→→ ←←

AARON GILBREATH

I spent my first year out of college lost. After graduating with a philosophy degree and a minor in ecology and evolutionary biology, I moved from Tucson, Arizona, back to Phoenix with my girlfriend and worked for my dad. He ran a thriving construction-related business from the second floor of my childhood home. Starting at 9:00 A.M., I sat at a desk in the spot where my bed used to stand, and I wrote paychecks and updated the company schedule. In the afternoon, I drove around Phoenix visiting jobsites. It was steady work that had a future in it, but not mine.

In my early twenties, Edward Abbey was my literary idol. Abbey wrote about the arid Southwest I knew and loved, and he turned his desert adventures, environmental values, and philosophical questions into fiction and nonfiction. That's what I wanted to do for a living. I just didn't know how to go about it.

Instead of creating time to practice writing each day, I avoided the grueling apprentice phase and languished in the comforting procrastination of the dreaming phase. I hiked, read, and watched TV. I told people my writing plans, but it was all talk. I enrolled in an elective university writing class and never attended. But amid all this fabrication, my real secret was heroin. I'd been snorting it every day during the months leading up to graduation, and the anxiety over my future, and the self-loathing I felt for not pursuing it, kept me snorting more. Heroin replaced fear with a false sense of serenity. I wanted to feel serene all the time.

Nobody knew about my habit, not my girlfriend or parents, not what was left of my old friends. I got high and went to dinner. I got high before work, and instead of writing, I stored the dream of my future self in the warm fog that heroin generated in the back of my head. Granted, I read a lot of books when I wasn't nodding off. And I journaled. Reading and journaling are essential steps to writing. But I didn't write— meaning, I didn't revise, and writing *is* revision. I outlined. I made notes and filled pages with bullet points for future stories I planned to compose one day, and that's where I stayed, in the planning stage. In the three years since discovering Abbey and my passion for prose, I finished college but never finished one story. My journal mirrored my life: it was all fragments and outlines for pending projects that went uncompleted and left me unfulfilled.

The more I avoided the work necessary to quit using heroin, the worse I felt about my future and about myself. Escapism is easy in that it puts you at rest, but that resting state can become harder to endure than the labor itself. Hard work is exhausting, but avoiding rewarding work is emotionally and psychologically draining. It starves the spirit. Better to get up and take the gratifying challenge. The exertion is fulfilling. It makes you feel good, the way you do after a long hike or strenuous run.

All of this is all easy to say in retrospect. During my first year after college, I just spun on the drugged hamster wheel. I worked for my dad. I hung out, and I sustained my habit. Until I got arrested for possession. Terrified and sweating in the back of the squad car, I remember telling the arresting officer, "This is just what I needed." I didn't want to keep on like this, numbing and procrastinating and squandering my abilities. I wanted action, wanted to feed rather than kill whatever fire burned inside me. My arrest forced me not only to deal with my substance abuse, but to confront my escapist behavior, of which drugs were the symptom, not the cause. Looking at a felony, I had to face the reality of my life: What had I made it into so far? What shape did I want it to take?

The time had come to see how badly I wanted this writing thing I kept talking about. Replace writing with your own passion or dream job—social work, activism, science, teaching— the story is the same: instead of running from the challenges that separate the current you from the dream you, run toward them. With time and help from family, mentors, professors, and friends, you will make progress.

As part of a diversion program, I stayed clean for a year, and Arizona law expunged my felony. Getting sober was easier than staying sober, which was why I got on methadone. Methadone offered incentives to abstain while I worked on changing my relationship with my mind, my free time, and my attitude. In order to dispense medicine, many modern clinics have firm rules. I used the rules as insurance. The longer methadone patients stayed clean, the more freedoms my clinic afforded, such as reducing weekly mandatory urinalysis to monthly urinalysis, and providing up two weeks' worth of takeout doses. This structure helped. As I reduced my dose, I thought hard about myself and behavior and focused on where I wanted to take things from there.

My girlfriend and I eventually parted, as we long sensed we would, and I moved to the Pacific Northwest. Alone in a damp climate, I thought I could finally establish the writing routine I'd failed to create in Arizona. When I moved, I put myself in a do-or-die situation. I could either spend the rest of my life talking about what I wanted to be when I grew up, or I could grow up and start fashioning myself into that person. I didn't want to be a heroin addict with an expunged felony who spent the rest of his life regretting his wasted potential.

In Portland, I started an indoor ritual: I sat at my computer in the morning before work and wrote for at least two hours. Every day I did this, including the weekends. Once I developed a healthy habit, the work became easier. Practicing wasn't as miserable as expected. It was challenging and fun. I fortified with tea and rewarded myself with chocolate, and, surprisingly, I looked forward to those mornings. As joy replaced fear, I made room for new friends, started taking day trips, and enjoyed exploring my city, because I no longer had something to run from and regret.

That's what I learned during my first year out of college: some of us screw ourselves out of options. We back ourselves into a corner that offers no alternative other than to do the one thing we know we need to do. After addiction and arrest, the life I wanted could have ended. But instead, it took the threat of nearly losing myself to give finding that life a try.

Domesticity 101

→» «←

JUSTIN WARNER

I started my freshman year of life when I was seventeen. Can you imagine a high school senior with an apartment? It was an AP class in disaster, but it also means that I've been at this for a while, and I have some things to say about getting started.

Let's talk about the domicile first. I am a full supporter of living alone if you can. Straight out of school, there is a huge part of your brain that you've barely even checked out, and that's the part of your brain that makes you do what you do when nobody else is around. Think about how much of your time you have spent helping other people navigate their lives and how much your life has been navigated for you by others. Take this freshman year to navigate yours, if you can, and not some drunk roommate's. It's easier to get the confidence you need in your entry-level job when you know that you are you and you aren't trying to be anyone else. The more time you spend with yourself, the more time you can perfect the art of you. That's the ticket out of entry-level existence.

I know you can save money by living with a roommate, but

I highly recommend taking on the cost if you can, depending on whether you live in a city where this is at all feasible. What you lose in money you will gain in long-term development.

That said, get a double bed. I said to live alone for the first year, but that doesn't mean someone can't come over for a protected roll in the synthetic down. Since you don't have a roommate's space to consider, and you have all of the above going for you, you are gonna be pretty darn attractive. But make a point to *not* find the ideal mate during your first year out of school. When you are in love, you make wacky decisions, and this is not the year for that. Fall in love next year. If you can't wait to fall in love for a year, then it probably isn't love in the first place.

Here are some ways to live alone, cheaply, and with a great deal of comfort.

Get blackout curtains for whatever room you sleep in, along with a real alarm clock, not your phone. When you control your sleep cycle, you will always be on.

Next, get one nonstick pan. Just one. This is only for eggs. A pan that only cooks eggs stays perfect and makes perfect eggs for a lifetime. Don't ever put anything else in it other than eggs or an omelet. Get a rubber spatula for manipulating your eggs. If you don't eat eggs, that's fine. But you may want to consider trying it just for this very formative year of your life.

You should also get a rice cooker with a timer. A rice cooker makes perfect rice without supervision and holds it at a safe and warm temperature without burning it all day. The timer means you can set it before bed and wake up to the smell of yummy rice. Your mind will say, *I should put an egg on that rice*, and you will, thanks to that nonstick pan. Eggs and rice are about the cheapest, most delicious things you could eat for breakfast, and I do it almost every day still. Put whatever condiments you've got floating around on there. I use hot sauce and furikake. I kick down doors at morning meetings and get asked to write things. That's the power of rice and eggs.

You should also get one simple, reliable cookbook. Cook a recipe, divide it into portions, and freeze the portions for later. You don't have to impress anyone with your cooking skills. You will be shocked how much of the food you cook exclusively for yourself is to your liking.

Always have a cheap bottle of red, white, or sparkling wine on hand. Often, the best memories are made from impromptu celebrations, which have a chicken-or-the-egg relationship with wine. Don't get rugs. You will spill wine on them.

When it comes to furniture, don't buy anything really good, really cheap, or really old. A very funny person once wrote those three things in a Venn diagram and determined that the middle was "your parents' furniture." I know I've been harping on becoming your own person during this year, but one final nudge from a relative wouldn't hurt. Trust me. There is a time to get IKEA everything, and it's not for your first place in your first year. Chances are you are going to want to move when your lease is up. You aren't making the dough to hire professional movers, and you will break your IKEA stuff in the move. This has happened to 100 percent of self-movers I know, myself included.

I don't know what else I'm qualified to tell you, other than to filter what people tell you to do with yourself. I can only tell you what I think would have worked best for me, looking back now, but despite failing to follow most of my own advice at the time, I'm not doing so badly, anyway.

Graduate School in Nebraska

AILEEN GARCIA

After college, I made one of the biggest decisions in my life and left the Philippines where I lived with my husband to move to Nebraska for graduate school. It's been almost a year since I came to the United States, and it's safe to say that I've never experienced such strong emotions, both positive and negative, in such a short length of time.

For the first few months, I felt like an infant needing assistance with everything, a child seeking a parent's affirmation that the world is a safe place. Back home, I'd had everything figured out. I didn't own much but had everything I needed. Add to that the strong, supportive relationships I'd built since childhood, and life was good. But choosing to start a new life in another country led me back to square one—I had to introduce myself again, start making friends, familiarize myself with a whole new place, and immerse myself in a culture I thought I wouldn't have trouble adjusting to. I'd go from feeling so blessed and confident to feeling unwelcome and unsure within an eight-hour period. Every day was a new emotional roller coaster. I knew it'd gotten really bad when, suddenly, Manila traffic seemed appealing to return to.

Back home, I was in a position where I could offer people help. Here, I found myself undeniably needing help and had to shamelessly ask for it. Each time, self-pity would creep in.

If I chose to be entitled, and wallow in my circumstances, I'd argue that pity was valid from all angles. Look with sympathy at this little Filipino woman who is homesick and alone, walks four blocks to the bus stop in the midst of freezing temperatures, who can't go anywhere outside the bus line, and doesn't even know how to cook. Poor girl . . .

(Okay, fine. The last one is just plain pathetic.)

But now that I feel the worst days are over (that's what I would like to believe, at least), the rational and grateful part of me insists that my self-pity is undue.

It hasn't been easy. I needed help almost on a daily basis. But thinking about it now, I realize, there was never a time that I didn't get help when I asked for it. Many times, I didn't even have to ask. And more often than not, I got more than I needed. Let this be my testimony of God's providence and how I'm a recipient of every type of kindness there is—from Filipinos and non-Filipinos alike—here in Nebraska.

Who would've thought that shortly after arriving in Lincoln, Nebraska, my sister would find out that her high school friend also lives here, a place many people dub to be in the middle of nowhere. Not only do we live in the same city, we live about six blocks from each other. Since the day we met, she has gladly offered to help me with everything, making life here so much more bearable. She's the one assisting me when I could very well be her older sister.

I lucked out with friends. They look after me and have taught me every little important detail about the university. They help me with my schoolwork and make me feel like I belong, lessening my longing for something familiar. They have become my voice of reason whenever I question my decision to come here. They encourage me when I miss my husband by saying, *"Time flies fast, he'll be here soon!"* I have delighted in talking with kind strangers while waiting for the bus, scouring for any tips in order to survive the upcoming winter or on how to better handle a long-distance relationship. I never knew how much a "Have a good day!" or "Keep warm!" remark could get you excited for what's ahead. Save for my daily FaceTime sessions with my husband, there are times when a short, lovely chat with a stranger is the only conversation I'll have all day.

I am blessed with caring professors, who, understanding the specific challenges in an international student's life, always check in on me and ask how I'm doing. When I was having problems with my lease after my husband came over, my advisor—who always goes beyond her academic duties—and her husband graciously offered their house to me and my husband for a month, just because they wanted to help. Not a room, but a house. Not a week, but a month.

I constantly find myself at the receiving end of kindness and hospitality, thanks to the wonderful Filipino crew here in Lincoln. They welcomed me into their homes, and not once have I felt I was being treated as a stranger. They are always ready to give me a ride, just to make sure I don't have to stay in my lonely apartment and miss our get-togethers. They always prepare Filipino food, its taste and smell capable of soothing each brewing nostalgia. They never fail to ask me if there is something I need, strongly refusing to let me pay for anything.

Their company and friendship, which I am tremendously grateful for, makes me feel like the Philippines are not too far away and that life in a foreign land is going to be all right. Like a dedicated and doting mother to a child, they give me two things when I ask for only one. When I ask for a small favor, they often give me all that they can give. It's the kind of generosity that is quite inexplicable, the kind that makes it feel like ten Christmas mornings in May.

What have I ever done to deserve such kindness?

I feel cared for and genuinely loved by these people.

And I thought I left family in Manila.

You'll Go

⇥⇤

KEVIN NGUYEN

When you graduate, some well-meaning but uninspired relative gifts you a copy of *Oh, the Places You'll Go!* It is a book made for children that has somehow become an acceptable thing to receive from someone who wants to acknowledge that you've made it to adulthood. "Congratulations," the accompanying card says, but you understand the subtext: "You graduated from college, so here is something you can enjoy at a first-grade reading level."

When you pack up your college stuff, you feel an irrational need to keep all your books. You're never going to crack open most of these books again—especially *The Norton Anthology of American Literature*, and definitely not *The Norton Anthology of American Literature Volume 2*—but you hang on to them, anyway. Even among the awkwardly sized textbooks, *Oh, the Places You'll Go!* is a pain to pack because it isn't the same shape as all your other books, the ones actually meant for grown-ups.

You keep a spreadsheet of every job you apply for. It becomes a depressingly large spreadsheet, and you remind yourself that

2009 is on the heels of a very bad financial crash, one you make sure to educate yourself on just enough to complain about. Eventually, you find your first job on Craigslist, where you'll make five dollars less an hour than you did at your work-study job. You cash your first paycheck and start to wonder if college would be the height of your career. At night, you write a lot. Occasionally, you publish your work online at websites that pay nothing.

Over time, you start to think wistfully about college. You reminisce about playing Frisbee on the quad, forgetting that you largely hated the kids who took Frisbee seriously enough to dub it with the modifier *Ultimate*. The memories of late nights drinking, of which you have no memory, somehow take the place of those when you stayed late in the library studying for finals. After your first postcollege breakup, you recall all those early romances seeming so innocent and carefree by comparison, even though it was mostly a lot of fumbling around for a condom in the desk drawer beside your twin bed. Frankly, you forget what college was really like.

After you luck into your first "real" job, as defined by its living wage, you feel like you've made it. In a moment of misguided confidence, you'll decide that the next generation of twenty-two-year-olds must hear your advice, that of a seasoned twenty-four-year-old.

The result is a book proposal for an anthology about life after graduation, much like the one you're reading. But it's not this one. A small publisher buys the proposal for a measly sum, offering you half of it now and half of it later. You commission all the pieces, edit them, and get saddled with the parody title *Oh, the Places You'll End Up Hanging Around*, which you don't hate but also don't love. It takes you months to assemble the book, waking up three hours before work every day for a summer to finish it. Several weeks after you turn in the final draft, the publisher notifies you that they've received a cease and desist from the Theodor Geisel Estate. (You Google *Theodor Geisel* and learn it's the real name of Dr. Seuss.) The publisher says they'll have to cancel the book, even when you remind them that the title was their idea. You never get the second half of the advance, and you pay the remainder of your contributors out of pocket.

To add insult to injury, your workplace will try to liven up the drab office environment by putting up tacky decals of famous quotes. One of them is, of course, from Dr. Seuss, though his name is somehow misspelled as "Dr. Suess." You correct it with a Sharpie.

When you move across the country to a big city, you throw away everything except a suitcase of clothes. Oh, and your books, nine boxes of which are kept in storage in the basement of a very generous friend's apartment. "I'll call for them when I'm settled," you say, which is a way of saying there's a good chance this move is a huge mistake and you'll be back soon.

Strangely, you are wrong. It is incredible how much better you feel after you've moved. The sensation is immediate, and though you are even poorer than you were before, new things seem possible. You make your first new friends since freshman year of college—a lot of them, in fact. You find a job you barely hate. You keep writing, and this time, people even pay you for it. It feels like a start of something, even though you're not quite sure what of.

At a party hosted by one of your new friends, you meet a cute stranger with a tattoo that says, "Kid, you'll move mountains." She's impressed when you correctly identify it as a line from

Oh, the Places You'll Go! Then you very smoothly tell her you hate that book more than anything else in the world. You're surprised that she gives you her number, but not surprised when she never texts back.

You wonder what kind of person gets an extremely trite Dr. Seuss quote inked on their body. A ridiculous person, right? *Right?* But then you start to question if there's really anything wrong with that. Maybe you're too judgmental! You wonder what kind of literary tattoo you might get and come up with nothing. You instead become very anxious at the thought of committing to anything permanent, that you might have to carry a single sentiment for the rest of your life.

Things in the new city are going well, and you get an apartment to yourself. You send for your books, which cost an exorbitant amount of money to ship across the country. The books, as it turns out, are too many to fit in your apartment. You don't have space for bookshelves, so the books are just stacked on the floor.

You go through your books. Pruning your collection is difficult for no reason. You get to *Oh, the Places You'll Go!* and wonder why you still have it. But you keep it anyway—the book written for children, the book with the cloying optimism that things will get better over time. You keep it because of all the places you've ended up hanging around, all the places you've been, and all the places you now know you eventually will go.

Down and Out in Boca Raton

JASON DIAMOND

I moved to South Florida two days after my final semester of college ended, living in the place where all of my relatives went when they retired, feeling like I was giving up in my early twenties. I'd run out of the little bit of money I had and didn't have any real plans to do anything with the rest of my life, so I occupied my father's guesthouse while I figured things out. All I wanted to do was order Chinese food and stare at CNN's "War on Terror" footage, the towers collapsing over and over, 9/11 perpetually cycling just above the news ticker on the bottom of the TV screen. Everything felt like it was falling apart, in my life and the world. I was frozen and not sure what to do.

After a month of neurotically wasting away and getting suspicious glances from the people coming back from tennis lessons on the rare occasion I left the guesthouse for supplies, I took my father's advice: "If you're not going back to school, at least do *something*." I applied for a job as a server at a local BBQ restaurant that catered to a mix of retirees, mostly from New York and New Jersey, and people that lived in the gated communities nearby. I got the job on the spot since there had been a lot of turnover recently. Three servers had enlisted, and another three had been poached by a competitor down the block. "I need good people," the manager said to me.

"I can be good," I told him, worrying that deep down I wasn't telling him the truth.

It was always busy at the BBQ place. The daytime lunch crowd was mostly made up of men in ill-fitting dress shirts and mismatched ties. They worked in the business park known around town for being the birthplace of the first PC. They talked about numbers and bottom lines, made jokes about their wives, and drank too much. Dinner customers were older people, sometimes brought in from the retirement home, other times visiting with their kids and reluctant grandkids. The most popular item on the menu was the pulled pork sandwich; we served up a few hundred of those a day. There was nothing too remarkable about that one sandwich. The meat was mealy, the tang from the sauce made my eyes water, and the soggy buns fell apart. There was a wall of hot sauces people could use to spice things up, but only if they signed a waiver saying that they absolved the restaurant of any responsibility.

Being a server isn't easy. You have to memorize daily specials, juggle plates, and sell yourself as much as you're trying to upsell diners on a pitcher of margaritas instead of just two glasses. ("It's Friday. I figured you could use this," the head server would say as he delivered pitchers to tables even if they didn't order it. The customers would get drunk and happy and never even say anything about the extra fifteen dollars on their bill.) Servers make sure the customers are always happy. "Anybody could do it," one of the servers told me as he counted out his tips, triple what I had made on that shift. "You can make a lot of money being good at bringing people lunch," he said.

The problem was that I was a terrible server who usually had time to kill while all of the others were busy making money. I spent my shifts hanging out in the kitchen and watching as the cooks did their thing. They yelled at each other in Spanish and answered back in Creole. I watched how they prepared the sandwiches, noted how their hands moved as they carved up the chickens, and piled a spoonful of baked beans onto every plate before calling, "Table ten, up." I thought about how that was where I should be, in the back with the cooks, that maybe that was the career for me. I memorized how they did each plate, thinking it didn't look that hard.

So when I saw my opportunity to work with them, on a busy lunch shift when they were down three cooks and getting slammed, I strutted past my manager, telling him, "I've got this," and jumped back behind the line. I was fast; I had flow. "Table three's getting cold!" I yelled at the smug head server. "These fries are getting a tan under the heat lamp," I cracked. Slinging sandwiches and collard greens on plates, it felt like I'd found my calling. I had figured it all out: I was going to be a chef.

Everything was going great for about ten minutes, and then I smelled something burning.

"Watch out!" the general manager yelled as he rushed past me with the fire extinguisher, spraying out a flaming pan behind me. I hadn't been paying attention. But it was too late; the smoke detectors started blaring, the sprinklers in the ceiling started going off, and the small grease fire I didn't notice stopped lunchtime work dead in its tracks. It wasn't my fault, but I was blamed for wasting hundreds of dollars' worth of pork and beef brisket because I was the person that wasn't supposed to be behind the line. "Get out! Now! *You're done!*" the general manager yelled, extinguisher still in hand. I didn't try to protest, didn't tell him it wasn't my fault. I nodded and walked out the door covered in barbecue sauce.

Later that night, after I scrubbed the smell of sauce and failure from my skin, I revisited my nightly ritual and turned on CNN. As I listened to some guy say people my age were the first group of new adults walking into a scary new world, I wondered how adulthood could not be scary. Maybe things weren't so bad for me. Sure, I was jobless and didn't have many prospects and was living in South Florida. But it was the beginning, and that meant the only place I had to go was up.

Walk-In Closet

→»«←

ALEXANDRA MOLOTKOW

I was scared to graduate. We were all scared to graduate. My whole student newspaper was so scared to graduate that editors stayed on for years, picking up and dropping half courses, living on production night leftovers and an honorarium the size of a freelance salary on a bad year—and 2008 was a bad year. The paper was like a job, which was better than no job, and there were no jobs.

The summer after I graduated, I got an internship at one of my favorite magazines and, by the kind of absurd luck you should never read into or extrapolate from, they needed a junior editor that fall. When the managing editor called me after the interview, I cried; it felt like a movie ending. *This is it*, I thought. *I've made it. I'm an adult!*

I was not an adult. I had no idea what an adult was. My notion of adulthood had everything to do with obtaining a job but nothing whatsoever to do with, say, cleaning the bathroom or taking out the garbage before it sprouted a white down of mold. On paper, I'd done okay, but I had no idea how to take care of myself. I'd been so wrapped up in boosting my employability that I'd neglected every other grown-up skill.

I found a studio apartment the size of a walk-in closet, in a sinking low-rise covered in cobwebs, not for lack of life but because no one ever bothered to sweep. In that building, it was appropriate to crank Black Sabbath at 3:00 A.M., or seat guests on a pile of socks, or cry for hours, or have room-shaking sex for hours, or yell at the wall for hours. My neighbors were mostly under thirty and worked either in bars or in media.

I didn't repaint or decorate; I figured I had other things to do, and also I didn't know how. I bought some vintage prints from an antique market and a couple of picture frames, but they didn't quite fit, so they sat on my bureau for months because I never bothered to look up the right way to dispose of glass. I never organized, so everything stayed in the last place I needed it. The apartment took on the impressions of my habits, until it was mine as much as a chewed wad of gum.

I never bought a bed; instead, I hauled over my childhood mattress, a twin, and dumped it on the floor. For months it seemed strangely indented, until a colleague pointed out it was upside down. Coworkers came over sometimes to drink and smoke indoors. They liked me; I reminded them of what they missed about their early twenties, as well as the reasons they were glad to have gotten them over with.

Work was going well. The less time I devoted to grocery shopping or bothering to pull my hair out of the shower drain before it coagulated into a mass the size of a rabbit impaled on a snake, the more time I had to practice editing—a life skill in itself, though it would be awhile before I applied it to my life. I didn't have a life. I thought I wasn't supposed to. Every night I came home from the office, heated up soup from a can (adding star pastina, for grown-up alphaghetti), and sat with an article until I cracked it. It always seemed impossible at first, so I chain-smoked and drank from economy-sized bottles of Georges Duboeuf Beaujolais. In those days, I could work while tipsy.

My older friends, at work and elsewhere, had spent their postcollege years backpacking through Europe, or tree planting in British Columbia—"finding themselves," and learning how to live. I did the reverse. My philosophy of life was mashing the keypad. I wanted to have fun, but I had to work, so I collapsed the two when I could and reinvested all my energy in my job.

One thing you should know is that dream jobs don't last forever. Either they stop being dream jobs, or you leave, and usually both. An unsung advantage to getting your dream job early is that it prepares you for disappointment. My job changed, and people I loved left, and the less happy I was at work, the more I realized that working hard at a job I loved had made me better company. I was a better listener, more understanding of others, and more useful to them. The more I liked the way I was at work, the more I wanted to be that version of me on my own.

I started learning how to take care of myself. It was hard, and it takes forever, literally, because it never ends. But I learned when it was time to learn. You can't do it all at once, no matter how much you think you ought to. Even successful people are failing at something.

Becoming a grown-up is not like jumping through a burning hoop. It's not just one hoop, and the process is nothing like jumping. It's more like untying knots, one after the other. Landing well after college is no guarantee you'll be landed at thirty, and feeling desperate at twenty-three doesn't mean you won't find success down the line, which will come with a new spread of complications. You'll succeed, fail, succeed, change fields, and, finally, learn to cook with ramen. You'll need every skill you accumulate.

Outsider/Insider

→» «←

JENNY ZHANG

I.

In eighth grade, in the middle of reading lines from Shakespeare's *Comedy of Errors*—a play my English teacher insisted was "funny if you would just put in the effort"—the two girls who sat behind me, who weren't even the worst of the worst, took out a box of packing peanuts and dumped its entire contents on my head. When I came home with little bits of white fluff in my hair, my grandmother exclaimed, "You've gone white!" in Chinese, and I mumbled, "It's freakin' Styrofoam!" in English and locked myself in my room, crying in that heinously dramatic way I had learned from watching my heroines on TV cry—the Lindsay Weirs and Angela Chases who seemed to have pain rumbling from their every pore, and yet, unlike me, they had friends who stood up for them, boys who tried hard to understand them, and a world that wasn't entirely hostile to every fiber of their being. I had packing-peanut pieces in my hair, a lifetime membership to the Itty Bitty Titty Committee, and the rest of my miserable life to dream about escaping a world that I swore could never, ever understand me.

When middle school ended, I scrawled in my yearbook, "MEMO: Eighth grade was hell. I hope Glen Cove burns down to hell. I was THE outcast," and subsequently spent the summer feeling lonely and abandoned, like a fleck of paint flung out to a part of the world without buildings or walls, someplace where my small, negligible life did not belong. "My life will always be like this," I wrote in one of my many notebooks that summer. If no one was going to talk to me, then I would talk to myself. If there was no one who I wanted to listen to, then I was going to listen to myself. That summer, I filled up eight notebooks with poetry and song lyrics that you couldn't tie me up and drug me into looking at again.

In ninth grade, I mixed sugar with water in my mom's spray bottle and used the mixture to spike my hair. It would be another year before I watched *SLC Punk!* and decided that I was a secret punker who was too good for the suburban hell I lived in. I was a misfit whose poetic sensibilities were just *too poetic* to ever be understood or accepted by the kids who traded last year's wide-legged JNCO skater pants for this year's Gap polos. I told myself that the kids who abandoned Green Day for Britney and would abandon Britney for whatever MTV told them to like the next year, who laughed at our seventy-five-year-old math teacher when she fell off her stool in the middle of explaining proportional fractions and then laughed at me when I went to help her get up, who prided themselves on how little they ever thought about anything and publicly shamed me for how much I always thought about everything, would grow up to be the kind of people who talked about high school like those were the halcyon days, like life peaked back then and would never be as good—and, for them, it wouldn't.

Just to keep myself from sinking, I had to believe that these kids, whose meanness and cluelessness were validated and encouraged by the entire structure of high school, would one day lead miserable, dreamless lives while I filled mine with poetry and rock and roll and adventure and love. And one day, I would return to this town that once gave me so much grief for not wanting to wear what everyone else wore and not wanting to cheat on tests like everyone else cheated on tests and not caring about sports or cheerleading or bake-sale fund-raisers or junior prom or senior prom or pep rallies or making fun of my teachers. I would roll through town and still be the weirdo I have always been, but instead of its being something grotesque, something to be attacked, it would be this dazzling, amazing thing. *Maybe I'm not too weird for this world*, I thought in ninth grade, hair sticky with sugar. *Maybe the world isn't weird enough for me.*

II.

And it wasn't. It just wasn't. I wrote angsty poems about feeling hellaciously black in a world of sunny, cheerful yellows. I briefly dated a boy who was the lead singer of a screamo band called—I crap you not—NINTH DEGREE BURN. He drew Xs in permanent marker on his wrists and layered black rubber bracelets over them. For Valentine's Day, he gave me a fake rose that he had dyed black, and I gave him two carnations like how you were supposed to do at funerals. All of my friends' screen names were like xNxOxOxOxIxWxOxNxT or like xXwishyou-weredeadXx. I started wearing clothes from my mom's closet, fun stuff like this white Heidi-of-the-mountains lace-up suspender skirt that had people yodeling at me in the hallways and asking if I was competing in the Ice Capades this winter.

I had a total of maybe four friends, none of whom I ever con-
fided in or spent time with outside of school, but they were
misfits, too. One of them had been misfortunately nicknamed
the Plumber because someone had spied her crack in shop
class; another wore her hair in a long, thick medieval braid
right down to her rump and pretended that our little suburban town in decline was really the Welsh countryside, sprawling and giving. Another was a practicing Wiccan whose mother
had pictures of naked, oiled rock stars in her house and once
lent me a black cape to wear, just 'cause.

As high school went on, I became bolder, more contrarian.
It seemed like I was one of four people in my school who read
books outside of class. I argued with my English teachers
whenever they insisted there was a "right" way to interpret a
text. I loved Joyce and Keats and Frost and Melville and Twain
and Woolf and Lawrence but resisted their place in the English
canon all the same. I disagreed openly with my teacher's
Freudian reading of *The Metamorphosis* and tried to formu-
late my burgeoning thoughts on feminism and racism while the
rest of the class was falling asleep or copying each other's
homework for the next period's class. My English classes turned
into one long dialectical conversation between me and my
teacher about literature and privilege and criticism. I stomped
around in platform combat boots and shredded sweaters and
my mom's old clothes that I rescued from the Dumpster.
On days when I just couldn't bear to step foot in my high
school, days when I knew I couldn't take it, I would skip school
and take the bus to Queens and then a subway to the East Vil-
lage because I harbored some absurd delusion that if I stood
outside Kim's Video in my combat boots and my shredded
clothes and my sugared hair that made me the target of

confused bees everywhere for long enough, I would eventually be swept up into a world of art and music and poetry. Deep down, as a fifteen-year-old misfit, I honestly thought that I would find my community just by standing around and doing nothing.

III.

But I didn't, and I was learning that standing around and doing nothing would not get you any closer to finding your place in the world. I had to do something. If everyone said I was weird, I thought, then maybe I *was* weird, and maybe I liked it, because I had to like myself if I was going to keep on living, and I wanted to keep on living, and if I wanted to keep on living, then I would have to like whatever it was about me that marked me as different from everyone else. So I embraced it. I did stuff with it. If I was a speck of paint in a world without walls, then I would build those walls myself. I convinced my parents to let me volunteer at a community center that put on punk-rock shows on the weekends, and I struck up a friendship with the director of the center, a forty-year-old former punker named Jim who gave me lists of movies to watch and introduced me to the Velvet Underground and Patti Smith and Television. When my dad brought home a crappy, old-school, dial-up modem that I wasn't allowed to use more than an hour a day because it made our phone lines busy, I spent that hour looking up profiles on AOL of people who liked Sylvia Plath poems and James Baldwin novels and listened to Jade Tree records, and put all of my energy into befriending them. I made friends with an anemic, sensitive, literary punker from Omaha,

Nebraska. We sent each other care packages filled with Polaroids and mixtapes, collages that he had made for me and poems that I wrote for him. I was alone, and I wasn't alone.

I spent my lunch period writing poems about escape and fantasy. I cut my hair short and dyed it burgundy. I applied to a summer program at Stanford University for high school students who wanted to spend three weeks intensively studying philosophy. I got in, and for the first time in a long time, I was happy. I felt like I belonged somewhere. I made more friends in three weeks than I had in five years. The first night, ten of us sat around in a circle talking about faith and our relationship to God and debated about abortion and the death penalty, and I explained how my atheism didn't deprive me of morality or purpose. We stayed up every night until four or five in the morning just talking talking talking, frantic that there wouldn't be enough time to learn everything about each other, and there wasn't. "I'll never be the same again," I wrote in my notebook on the plane ride back to New York. And I wasn't. My suspicion that there was space for me in this world had been confirmed, however fleetingly, and I thought maybe if I could just get through high school and escape my miserable town, then I would continue to find these spaces already inhabited by others who had made the same pilgrimage that I wanted so badly to make.

I approached my last year of high school with a level of misanthropy that I find embarrassing now. When I was voted "Most Individual," it felt like a backhanded compliment coming from my classmates, who systematically tore down individuality and championed conformity. I watched and taped religiously every single episode of *Freaks and Geeks* on my

VCR, regularly staying after class to trade recaps and commentary with my English teacher, who identified as the "geek" to my "freak." I fell to the floor, overcome with vindication, when in the last episode the AV teacher drew an imaginary graph for Sam, Neal, and Bill, illustrating the rise and decline of the high school jocks and popular girls who would never know glory again after high school, whereas the freaks, geeks, and cretins would steadily rise. *I just have to wait*, I thought. *I just have to wait until I graduate from high school, and then I'm gonna get the hell out of here.* I knew my people were out there, scattered like I was scattered, and somehow I was gonna traverse this fucking amazing universe and find each and every one of them, and we would be one another's barrier to the horrific outside world that did not love us, did not appreciate us, and did not care that we spent the first seventeen years of our lives so utterly alone.

IV.

When I was ten, my legs grew too long too fast, and I was so bony that it hurt me to lie down on the mats in gym class. My mom told me that growing happens only when you're asleep, so for weeks I tried to stay up and watch over my legs, hoping to stop them from growing, and for a while, I thought it was working. "I'm not growing anymore," I said to my mom. "Bullshit," she said in Chinese. "You're ten years old; you can't stay this size forever." And I didn't; the growing happened despite my efforts.

The jabs and the jokes about my knobby knees and my next-to-nothing chest that were so much a part of the early years of my teenage life, that I thought I would carry in my heart forever like a wound that does not heal, disappeared one day. It took me some time to catch up with these changes, to switch my idea of myself as this awkward, gawky, hideously unwanted creature to someone who didn't need to move through the world so wounded all the freaking time. And no matter how much I tried to track these physical changes—to the point where I would sometimes spend entire afternoons sitting in front of a mirror, waiting to see something happen—it always came as a surprise. Like the time I walked past my university's post office and saw my reflection in the glass door and I felt so beautiful and happy that I wanted to cry, because the day had finally come when I had realized that I was no longer the person I was when I thought the pain I felt would be the pain I would always feel.

V.

But how do you do it? How do you even get started? That was my question when I was thirteen and picking Styrofoam out of my hair. "How do you build a house from scratch?" I asked my father, who told me, "You just do. You pick up a brick and you just start."

"And how do traffic jams happen?" I asked him. "How does an entire highway get backed up for miles?"

"It just does," he said. "And it always starts with someone."

"But how does one person start a jam that affects like ten thousand other people in their cars?"

"You just do it," my father told me, as if it were just that simple. As if all you had to do was just start doing anything at all, and eventually your little actions would become huge.

Once my father and I were driving on Grand Central

Parkway, where oversize trucks aren't allowed because the overpasses are too low, and we saw this huge truck enter the highway. My father said to me, "He's going to get stuck," and sure enough, after a few minutes, the truck had gotten stuck underneath an underpass. We were right behind the truck, so we were the first car to slow down to a halt. "Look behind us, Jenny," my father said. I looked behind us and saw all the cars that had slowed down and stopped. "We just started a traffic jam."

At some point, I just started. I read all the time and I wrote all the time and I listened to music I loved and I sought out people who I thought might know about music and books that I would love, too. I rigorously researched colleges and universities to find ones that had strong creative-writing programs. I got into Stanford after spending months on my college applications, spilling my guts out into my personal essays; and at Stanford, I took every poetry and fiction class I could, joined every club that seemed even a little bit interesting, went to every reading I heard about or had time for in my schedule, met people who made art and played music, and started a writing group with my friends that still exists today, only now we are all published authors and journalists and novelists and poets. I applied for grants that allowed me to travel to Paris two summers in a row and spent six weeks obsessively researching the literary and artistic community in Paris, and when I got there I immediately went to Shakespeare and Company, the bookstore that Allen Ginsberg and William Burroughs and Anaïs Nin once frequented, the bookstore that famously offered beds in exchange for poems, where I was determined to sleep among the books I had spent my whole life reading, and it turned out, all I had to do was show up with my big dreams balled up in my sweaty fists and ask if I could spend the night. The answer was yes.

I spent my first summer in Paris tirelessly and relentlessly seeking out miscreants and weirdos, and came back the next summer to continue where I'd left off, hanging out with the crust punks from Germany, falling in love with a Swedish boy who had walked on a bed of hot coals, writing poetry on Pont des Arts, and flirting outrageously with boys and girls who found my social awkwardness lovable instead of execrable.

I'm twenty-eight now, old enough to know better—old enough to shed my old attachments to this idea of being the ultimate loser, the unknowable weirdo—but I'm still clinging. I can't let go of the scared, angry, alienated seventeen-year-old I was when I went off to college in California, where everyone was always "SO AWESOME" and so happy and so cheerful and so upbeat and I was always so "mysterious" (EW) and "artsy" (EW) and "quirky" (EW EW). I can't let go of that girl, even though at some point, I was so proud to be myself and so alienated by everyone else that I started to work really hard to find people who would never use the word *artsy*; and then I found them, and I started to date boys who didn't think I was "quirky" but just got who I was; and slowly, painfully, and ignorantly, I began to accept that things were changing. Maybe *I* wasn't changing, but my idea of who I was needed to change. I couldn't cling to my old safety net of "everyone is against me!" because the happy, creative bubble I wanted for myself was happening, and in order to love it, in order to experience it, I had to acknowledge it.

So here I am, acknowledging it. Acknowledging that a few

weeks ago, I went on a poetry-and-puppets tour with the poet
Zach Schomburg and the multimedia puppet troupe Manual
Cinema. We spent a week driving down the East Coast in a Ford
Econoline, listening to the songs I listened to when I thought
I would always live on the edges of everyone else's world, except I wasn't on the edge anymore; I was right there in the
center. I was still the cheerful, moody, puerile, poop-and-
farts-obsessed wannabe poet I had always been, except I was in
a van with other poets and musicians and actors and trapeze
artists and puppeteers—the very people I had hoped to meet
standing on the corner of St. Marks and Third Avenue—and
every day we drove to a new city where we shared the things we
made with people who had come to hear poetry, and there
were nights when I stood there, trembling, with poems in my
hand, wondering, *How did I get here?*

I got here because I *had* to get here. As soon as I stopped
standing on corners, I began to find other misfits and explor-
ers. So here I am, in it. Acknowledging it. Loving it. Wanting
you to know that as much as it might look like nothing is happening right now, as much as you might think that it's possible for a person to be this lonely forever, in fact, slowly, bit by
bit, the dust that has been gathering in your corner will clear,
and one day, when you are returning to your lonely place for
the hundredth or thousandth time, you will be surprised to
find that the dust is gone and there in your corner of the world
will be people like you who have been waiting for you this
whole time as much as you have been waiting for them.

Homebody

→»«←

MIRA GONZALEZ

Drop out of school and move back in with your parents at the start of your third year of college. Your parents don't approve, that much you can tell, but they don't voice their disapproval, either. Not yet. Try not to leave your new makeshift bedroom, which is actually a large closet in the living room, because your younger sister has completely taken over the room you used to share. Leave your door open most of the time, but only a crack, to let some light in and so your family won't think you are avoiding their company. Rather, your family will assume that you are "working" and do not want to be disturbed unless it's absolutely necessary. Actually, your family will definitely not assume you are working until you tell them, repeatedly, every time someone opens your door, that you are working. But still, do not close your door. That might give your family the impression that something is wrong, which could potentially lead to a conversation about why you are closing them off, and that is exactly the kind of unimaginably nightmarish situation that you organize your life around avoiding.

In order for your family to believe you are working, you must maintain the façade of a nebulous and likely nonexistent career path that mainly involves work you can do from bed. Tell them you are a freelance writer or an electronic musician. When people ask you how you spend your days, tell them you "mostly just work." Make sure this is a job where nobody can track your progress.

Do not go out with friends; do not be social. This causes you too much anxiety now. Instead, invent an elaborate lie about how being in social situations usually makes you feel guilty, because you aren't at home working, which is true to some degree. You do feel guilty for not working, you wished you worked harder, but secretly you suspect that you lack the skill and discipline to succeed in your given field. You would rather constantly feel guilt for not working hard enough than deal with the undeniable failure of working hard and not succeeding.

Consume everything you possibly can: food, drugs, books, movies, television, sex. Do not, however, under any circumstances, experience these things fully. You may only consume in the most efficient way possible. Consume as much as you can while exerting the least possible amount of effort and no self-awareness. Eat food with your hands while standing in front of the refrigerator. Always choose pills over smokable or sortable drugs. (Pills are easier, more reliable). Movies and television should only be watched in bed on your laptop using a Netflix account that your ex-boyfriend's parents pay for.

When you do (rarely) have sex, it should be with virtual strangers. Have the kind of sex that seems great while you're intoxicated but causes you to sneak out of their apartment the next morning feeling horrified at yourself. It is important to show little or no emotional investment when finding a sex partner in order to completely eliminate all opportunities for rejection. For this reason, only have sex with whomever seems most available to you. If you have to make any effort at all, then it is not worth it.

Always be agreeable in all interactions, whether with friends, family, ex-romantic partners, drug dealers, or grocery store employees. Never say anything that might upset someone; never be the kind of person that anyone could dislike for any logical reason. Always be polite, always be empathetic. Ask questions, make eye contact, be charismatic. You know that your personality is not naturally this way. You are not charming or likable in reality, but by pretending you are, you can avoid any type of exhausting conflict or criticism that might happen if you were to speak your mind. This pattern of behavior is obviously incredibly exhausting and entirely unsustainable; therefore, you may not remain in any social situation for more than an hour or two. Otherwise, you could accidentally slip into a pattern of behavior that will lead people to believe you are the boring, unlikable person that you actually are.

Be self-deprecating to the point where people can identify with you, but not to the point where people feel alienated or confused by you. Never, under any circumstances, should someone feel bad for you, or feel sympathy for your situation. There should be no situation, as far as anyone else is concerned. Everyone should think you are the regular amount of sad and unproductive for any human in your general age range. Therefore, you should always downplay what you are really feeling. It is important to keep in mind that any mentally healthy person will feel approximately half of the negative emotions that you are experiencing, which means that you should always take half of your feelings and hide them from every living being on the planet, if possible. If that does not feel possible, do not leave your room. I repeat, do not leave your room.

Desire insane amounts of validation from people, but never actively seek it. Have desires, but never express them, then become upset when people don't fulfill your unvoiced desires. Become disillusioned with the world, with relationships, and with humanity as a whole when you are treated poorly by someone you trusted. A non-stranger you made the mistake of having sex with. Someone you foolishly hoped had enough patience to love you. Feel wronged when they don't do the things you want them to do, even though you never told them what you wanted. Wonder why every person in the entire world seems inevitably separate from you at best and in some kind of malicious plot against you at worst.

Never stop anyone from doing anything that bothers you. Your self-esteem is low enough at this point that you feel you have not earned the right to ask anything of anyone. You don't think you deserve anything but less-than-ideal treatment from others. Allow this feeling to stay with you for years. However, you should occasionally put yourself under the impression that, maybe one day, using patience and empathy, or a small amount of telepathy, someone will figure out exactly what you want without you having to say anything. In turn, become frustrated when nobody seems to be able to please you, but still, never impose your own desires onto others. You do not have enough self-worth for that.

Listen to friends talk about how when they are depressed, they swing unpredictably between being manically productive and extremely unmotivated. Realize that your depression only ever results in the latter. Wonder why your depression has to be different from and shittier than other people's depression.

Begin to feel like something is horrifically, irreparably wrong with you, and that you are a profoundly inept person for not going through phases of extreme productivity when you are depressed. Convince yourself that you are doing depression wrong. Say things like "Yeah, me, too!" when your friends talk about being productive while depressed, then regurgitate what you heard in future conversations. Tell people that you sometimes become manically productive when you're depressed, despite knowing for a fact that's not true. Begin to wonder if other people were lying about that, too, and if everyone is just depressed and unproductive and lying about it because they are insecure in their depression, too. For a moment that will inevitably pass too quickly, allow yourself to feel grateful and not alone.

PART THREE

→»«←

Love and Relationships

Staying in Touch

→» «←

SAM ZABELL

I'd heard it from other people a million times, but I still couldn't believe how alone I felt my first year out of college in New York City.

The subways and streets were constantly crowded—so crowded, in fact, that elbows to the rib cage or accidentally stepping on heels had become commonplace on my commute. Stores seemed to be open 24-7. And yet, as I walked to work or to the grocery store or even to a bar to meet coworkers or old schoolmates, I felt unbelievably alone.

People were probably tired of hearing that "all my friends live in Chicago" for many reasons, most notably because it wasn't true. I did have a nice circle of friends in New York—some coworkers I'd become close with, and other close friends who were ahead of me in school and acted as my guides in this city they'd already been settled in for two years. I was not technically alone, but I was without friends who shared my experience. I was handling the unfamiliarity of the real world by myself, while the bulk of peers my age leaned on each other in Chicago, roomed together, opened tabs for each other at bars, included each other in plans, and continued to support one another with just their physical presence. I was alone in New York by those standards, in my own time zone, with a costly apartment, an intimidating new job, all in a city I was not used to navigating. *They are so lucky*, I thought. *They'll forget about me. They don't get what I'm going through.*

Keeping in touch with friends wasn't simple. A "like" on Instagram or a view of a Snapchat story does not constitute actual connection, although it does keep you in the loop. Before, it felt easier to keep in touch with high school friends because we had the experience of college in common. We'd understand the dramas of the hookup culture, the pressure of recruiting season, the hilarity of a long night out that ends in 2:00 A.M. pizza orders, the stress of midterm exams. But life after college doesn't follow that same rubric. Every job is unique; the term *entry-level* signifies a wide range of responsibilities across industries; our apartments are different sizes, in different neighborhoods. To truly keep in touch meant I needed to make time to not only catch up on the big things, but also to familiarize myself with the minutiae of my friends' day-to-day existences. Perhaps it would've been easier to get a blueprint of their apartments and a roster of their coworkers so I could internalize the data and picture where they were.

I've heard all kinds of advice on how to stay in touch over the phone: consider the time sacred, take the time to sit and listen; don't talk to them in the ten minutes between your apartment and the subway, or as you wait for the elevator; don't simply text to say, "What's up?" because it will inevitably be answered by, "Not much, you?" I was lucky enough to have a forty-five-minute walk to work, both ways, for the first year in New York. Okay, I wasn't sitting down when I called my friends, but I had almost an hour to devote to them multiple days a week. Texting wasn't enough. Phone calls, where I could hear voices and laughter and emotion, those were how I really stayed in touch.

Of course, friends fade. Everyone will not be your friend forever, but I learned the difference between deep friendships and peripheral friendships. Peripheral friends will take you to lunch when you visit their city; they may even let you crash on the couch. Intimate friendships will take crying phone calls or send you a plane ticket for your birthday so you can spend it with them in Chicago (true story).

I found my way forward, ironically, by going back to "old" methods of connection. Make phone calls and send birthday cards. Reach out with bits and pieces of you—your voice and your handwriting—to let them know you care about them. A text before a presentation is helpful, an e-mail is good, but nothing will reassure you like a phone call. Don't worry if you can't say, "It's like nothing's changed!" Everything changes after college, but change is good, and you will change together.

Somewhere Between Mountains

SKYLAR KERGIL

Freshman year of college, I fell in love with my best friend. I did a whole lot of nothing about it until a few months before she was going to study abroad for our entire junior year. When I did finally tell her, I was relieved to hear she felt the same, but long distance? No way, we said. Still, somehow, some way, we ended up together for that year, and senior year, and through graduation, with hopes of going on to forever . . . the sort of forever that feels like whatever perfect means, you know?

Anna was always more academically driven than I, so it came as no surprise that she'd already figured out what she wanted to do after school—to work on a farm and then begin a program working as a food coordinator and educator with a local organization in Montpelier, Vermont. Meanwhile, I packed up my studio art degree along with my oil paints, tools, and plywood to move back in with my mom until I figured out how I could join her. I eventually decided to put that degree to maximum usage by applying to become a bank teller at a bank near where Anna would be working. Actually, it turned out to be in the same building. Small world.

Anna had rented a tiny bedroom from a woman with two young kids in a farmhouse just outside the tiny capital of this beautiful state. When I began my job interviews, I was mainly living out of my car with my brand-new set of shirts, ties, pants, and shoes that turned me from looking like the twenty-two-year-old hippie that I was into a slightly serious young professional. Pretty sure I joined the Young Professionals of Montpelier Facebook group as well. Pretty sure I'm still a part of it, actually.

After an interview with a local bakery, I popped over to the bank and realized, just a few moments before walking in, that the nose piercing I'd gotten with one of my best friends in college may not be appropriate. I pulled it out in the middle of Main Street. Now that my face was looking legitimate for the job, I covered the tiny bird tattoo I had given myself on my thumb when I was fourteen with a Band-Aid and awaited the questions about my résumé.

"Oh, you have done public speaking? What kind?" asked my future boss. I took a deep breath and launched in, "Well, you see, I'm transgender and have been publicly transitioning from female to male since I was seventeen and advocating for . . ." I trailed off as I read the smiles from both of the people interviewing me. "That's so interesting! How cool!" was essentially their response. Amazing!

Within a few weeks, I was working, and Anna and I had found a cheap basement apartment that allowed cats. Things settled, like the dust on the wall-to-wall carpeting, and I brought my fifteen-year-old cat, Tiger, over to move in. Tiger loved Vermont, Anna and I loved each other, and all seemed perfect. Except for one major thing: now that we were living together, people began to insinuate or downright ask, "So . . . when are you getting married?"

Falling in love with my best friend was incredible. It had taken me so long to work up the courage to ask her out for a variety of factors. She identified as straight, and I am a transgender man who, growing up, had been bombarded with society's relentless messages that I was unlovable. While Anna hadn't had many serious relationships before we got together, I had been in back-to-back monogamous ones out of the fear of being alone. Anna's love showed me not to fear any longer, and without that fear, I began to think about the future. We felt much too young to get married. I hadn't spent any time alone to practice self-love. She wanted to travel and move around the country, whereas I wanted to relocate to Boston and pursue my music and activism more thoroughly.

After years of being taught that true love was possessiveness, was like "owning" another person (i.e., "you are mine" or "you are my everything"), I realized that true love was not claiming another's life as your own. True love, I learned with Anna, was unconditional support for whatever a person needs or wants to do with their wild life. For us, true love manifested as the ability to see one another's dreams, support them wholly and selflessly, and when our paths began to diverge, listen as love told us to let go.

We knew we would be moving out separately almost eight months before we actually did. It didn't make it easy, and the hardest part was trying to explain it to others. We were still very much in love until the day she moved out. In the spring, she would listen to rough drafts of the songs I was writing about us ending—she still enjoyed them and being a part of my process. After she left in early summer, I had a week before moving down to Boston of just Tiger and me floating through a space that had been my first adult home. I was lonely. I cried myself to sleep. I wondered if we would regret our decision. I wondered if I had just traded my soul mate for some selfish dream. I wondered if she was happy, if she would be okay, if this truly was a balanced and joint decision.

It has been over a year now, and Anna and I are still friends. We have had many amazing experiences both together and apart in these past few years that we wouldn't have had if we hadn't taken that leap. I don't know if or when or to whom I will ever get married, but I know that if she does, I will be so thankful to attend her wedding. It will be gorgeous, perhaps in a field or a farm somewhere tucked between mountains, and she will look beautiful.

Dude of the Year

→←

SARAH MIRK

A dozen of my new best friends crowded around the Thanksgiving table. We didn't own many chairs, so the seating arrangements were motley and wobbly— bar stools, a piano bench, a sofa dragged over from the living room where I sat, sinking into the cushions with a plate of Tofurkey precariously balanced on my knee, gesturing as I told an elaborate story about having sex with two different guys on the same night. This was a convivial, degenerate storytelling competition.

After graduation, I'd moved into a house off Craigslist with four guys I didn't know. Now, we were fast friends and had christened our home the Dude Ranch. Around the Thanksgiving table, someone had suggested we anoint an award: Dude of the Year. Each of us launched into stories extolling our dudeliness, and as I finished my narrative with a flourish ("And in the morning, we drank the extra beer for breakfast!"), the table burst into applause. The judges' convening was brief: just six months out of college, I was officially Dude of the Year.

But over the next few days, the award gnawed at me. Why

had I wanted to show off my exploits, anyway? Talking up myself as a freewheeling libertine had left me feeling a little, well, gross.

In February of my senior year of college, I broke up suddenly with my lovely boyfriend, citing both irreconcilable differences and a desperate need to have sex with a bunch of other guys. We'd been dating for almost all of college, and I was obsessed by the idea that I was missing out on crucial life experiences by limiting myself to only one person. I disconsolately saw myself as a bit of a naïve country mouse—I vividly imagined that sleeping around would make me a worldlier, more sexually sophisticated individual. So with ninety days to go until graduation, I severed my romantic ties and dedicated myself wholeheartedly to sleeping my way through campus.

My guiding principle was to "act like a guy." Whereas before I was romantic, largely sober, and into talking about feelings, now I would be proudly slutty, down for a party, and emotionally aloof. I'd say yes to anything (Smoking pot out of an apple? Let's do it! Filling an entire aquarium with vodka Jell-O and My Little Pony figurines? Amazing!) and to pretty much anyone. I wouldn't worry about my reputation. I wouldn't get sincere. I wouldn't get anxious about my body. I would be unattached and unapologetic. Women carry around a lot of baggage about being respectable, about being sexy without being sexual, about being emotional caretakers. To hell with all that! I'd be a dude instead.

The next six months were a whirlwind. Through the end of college and then onto my new life in a new city with a whole new group of friends, I put the moves on any guy I was remotely attracted to. If I liked a guy and we were hanging out alone, I'd straight up ask, "Hey, want to make out?" Almost always, they said yes. I had sex on my sink. I had sex on a giant trampoline. I had sex with a guy who I later found out was known around town as "Slackjaw." I was the person I had fantasized about being back when I was in my serious relationship.

But by Thanksgiving, things were a little rough.

While the table toasted my dude-dom, I actually wasn't drinking. I had to lay off alcohol because I was on antibiotics to treat a kidney infection. I'd met this unemployed carpenter while having lunch in a vegan café, and though his demeanor had raised several red flags—rather sleazy, constantly talking about his anarchist politics but seeming to have lot of money from a vague trust-fund-like source—I invited him over a few nights later, and we had sex. The next morning, I woke up with a wicked UTI that quickly spread to become debilitating. It was a nasty wake-up call from my body. While I could feign nonchalance, sex was always more complicated than I wanted it to be. Sex had repercussions—emotional and physical. Swapping bodily fluids is serious business, as much as I longed for it to remain casual.

Not to mention, all the devil-may-care sex I was having wasn't actually very good. It turns out sex wasn't fun for me when I was trying to be cool. Aspiring to be "chill" meant biting my tongue a lot. It meant brushing off my instincts, ignoring bad feelings when they came up, and refusing to utter honest compliments, afraid they might come off as too squishy or girlfriend-y.

So there I was: a self-made Dude of the Year. My award was a glassful of bladder-friendly cranberry juice, a round of prescription antibiotics, and a second date with an anarchist carpenter who I didn't even like. Looking back on it, I realized my lifestyle had left a wide wake. While I decided I'd be emotionally unattached, the guys I made out with often hadn't made that choice. When they brought up feelings, I shut them out. When they expressed anxiety about their bodies or vulnerable uncertainty about their desires, I told them to chill out, man.

I looked around at the actual dudes of the Dude Ranch. They weren't acting like me at all. While they were happy to cheer on my hookups, they often took things slowly with girls they liked. They were kind to the people they dated. The reason we'd become such good friends is because they were all often open about their feelings. We could get real. In acting like a guy, I'd been embodying a macho, masculine stereotype that was just as retrograde as the modest femininity I'd been trying to escape. I wasn't being fair to myself or to the guys I slept with—I wasn't being a dude, I was just being an asshole.

Over the next year, I didn't try to act like a guy. Instead, I tried to act a lot more like myself. That didn't mean embracing monogamy—but it did mean making more space for feelings. It meant listening to my partners' ideas and anxieties, even if we were just casually hooking up. It meant apologizing when I hurt people and speaking up when I was sad. It meant being okay with saying no instead of yes.

Angels That Get Us from Here to There

↠↞

GALA MUKOMOLOVA

O ften, I sleep over at my friend's house in her too-hot lofted bed in her tiny room. There are sufficient reasons why. First of all, my friend is an artist. She lets me use her supplies long hours into the night: watercolor marker-brushes, metallic ink, and heavy-grain paper. She observes my progress with a generous precision. "Think about the bottom of the blue jar, how the glass has its own light," she says. I think about it, and then I ask her to show me. But there is another reason I stay over. For lack of a beautiful word, we're both sad. Sad, the ways many young people these days are sad, functionally lost and leaking talent into unfathomable black holes. It is sometimes easier to be sad together.

I didn't mean to tell you so much so soon. What I was getting to, in my roundaboutness, was the package awaiting me when I returned home from my friend's apartment. I had been expecting it, an envelope, brown and without much decoration, from my former college advisor, Betty. She had e-mailed me asking for my new mailing address. Still, when I opened the envelope and held the contents in my hands, I was moved.

Pristine cardstock, white with black lettering, twenty sheets held by a translucent band. Prose poems by Mary Ruefle, each a meditation on one color of sadness. When Ruefle talks about the color blue, she describes it as a sweetness that's been cut into strips.

Something like eight years ago, less than a year after I graduated college, Betty sent me a small blue envelope. Hidden inside a nondescript greeting card were two checks, two strips of sweetness amounting to $400 from her and her partner, Susan. At the time I was living on nothing in Oregon, offering arts and crafts classes to kids in underfunded schools and performing volunteer puppet shows that explained depression to children. One night, after I'd spent a long day gluing sticks to other sticks, Betty got me on the phone. She wanted to know how life was out there in the Northwest, how I was doing post-graduation with my very valuable women's studies degree. Unwittingly, I let slip the fact that I was in dire need of a root canal and two crowns. "How are you going to pay for that?" she asked, knowing the answer was "With difficulty."

Jews don't really believe in heaven or hell, but we believe in angels. Angels that get us from here to there, *Second Sex* to *Gender Trouble*, subsidized loan to scholarship, tumult to awe. In my bright-eyed days as a college student, Betty was my angel. I didn't know that then, of course. When she magically increased my tuition funding or let me slink into her office and weep while she played "Girl on a Road" by Ferron (Canada's other Leonard Cohen), I imagined she took her role as the director of the women's studies department very seriously. In reality, Betty was one of the few adults in my life who could see through my pride to a girl who was learning to navigate the world without any sort of real emotional or financial support.

I never cashed those checks; I tucked them back in their card for safekeeping instead. Oral surgery was expensive, and I got an installment plan to pay for it. It wasn't the worst thing, taking care of myself. What Betty gave me was bigger than cash; it was a reminder that I wasn't flying without a net even if I looked down and saw only the hard ground.

The envelope of Mary Ruefle poems was followed by an e-mail from Betty. It read: *Did you receive the poems/meditation by Mary Ruefle? Seem like a prayer flag to you?* I pictured Tibetan prayer flags, how they are arranged by color, how they evaporate in the sun and offer their wise love up to the air; generous and across great distances. It took me a few days before I could reply. *Dear Betty,* I wrote. *Your friendship is a prayer flag I carry with me everywhere.*

Everything Is Fine

JAMIE LAUREN KEILES

You are a good person. If you are not a good person, you can start becoming one right now by just behaving as a good person would behave next time you are called to make a decision. If you are not sure if you are a good person, take comfort in the fact that it is not your responsibility to reflexively determine what kind of person you are.

Your friends like you. You do not have too many shallow acquaintances. In the event that you do have too many shallow acquaintances, the only way to rectify that situation is to accumulate history together via the passage of time until you are intimate friends. Time is already passing, so you are already doing everything you can do. If this is not a satisfying answer, just say yes to one extra social plan this week to create for yourself the illusion of action.

Everything in your past already happened, and there is nothing really you can do about it. Unburden yourself from the obligation to constantly fight against unchangeable bygone situations. This is not lazy—it's just the only thing you can actually do. Strive to do better in the future, and not in some grandiose, compulsive way. Just try to make the small, good choice every time you are presented with a new choice to make.

You do not need to think about whether you should go to graduate school today. You have already missed most deadlines for the year, so that recurrent tangent can be shelved once again until at least June. You may put an event on your calendar now to remind you to resume considering it then. Additionally, your life would not be better if you moved to a new/different city. Your life would be marginally more exciting for a few months due to the stress and thrill of moving, and then it would eventually be the same because you are the only constant in your life. Everything is fine. No ambitious action is required at this juncture.

You can re-up on goals at any time. You can restart your day at any time. If you have failed at something you were trying to do, or soured your day too soon with depression, you can restart from the beginning at any moment. Improvement doesn't hinge on circadian rhythms. Just go in the bathroom and close your eyes for a second and come back out and restart your day. A goal you set at 11:23 A.M. or 9:45 P.M. doesn't have worse odds than a goal you set when your alarm clock goes off in the morning.

Do not think about winter as one long, dense block of grayness. Just take each day in chunks of a few light-gray hours. Keep in touch with friends. Cook something in a big pot. Watch a movie you've been meaning to watch. Leave the house. Go on a walk. It's free!

Everything is fine!

I'd Rather Die Than Ask for Help

→»«←

CARVELL WALLACE

I don't like being told what to do. I never have. I also don't like needing to be told what to do. I don't like it when people say, "Hey, have you thought of this?" "Yes, I thought of it," I say while thinking of it for literally the first time. I don't like it when people say, "You seem stressed," or "Need some help with that?" I dislike advice so much that I've developed super-human abilities to detect when people may even *possibly* be giving me some no matter what they're actually saying. Like bat ears but for my ego. Someone could say, "There's a parking spot over there," and my first thought is *What? You think I don't know what a parking spot looks like?*

I grew up with a fair amount of what you might call chaos. Much poverty. Periodic evictions. The occasional bout of homelessness. My mother, God rest her soul, was a lovely, charismatic, and entirely batshit-crazy woman whose grip on reality was tenuous even on her best days. Whenever some drama would jump off—the car would get repossessed, I'd come home from school to the news that we needed to find someplace else to live by midnight tonight, I'd wake up in the morning and emerge from my room only to be greeted by LAPD in our apartment arresting her for larceny and bad checks—I would rely on what I thought was my very own superpower: the ability to be infinitely insouciant. Entirely unbothered. *Whatever,* I would think. *We're all going to die, anyway. I'm having cookies for breakfast.*

I thought it made me cool. Other people had drama. Other people couldn't handle it when things went sideways. But I was made of entirely different stuff. I was an artist and a philosopher, and I could be quietly bemused while everything went to shit around me.

This might have been a totally awesome way to be if only it weren't an elaborate ruse designed to mask a roiling undercurrent of helplessness, terror, and panic. I was afraid that if I started feeling things, I would never stop. I was panicked that if I needed help, there wouldn't be any. But most deeply, I was convinced that if I was not completely unassailable at all times, completely cool no matter what happened, then I wouldn't be lovable. I was afraid that if people knew I needed help, then they wouldn't love me.

Let's be honest. The need to be loved drives almost everything we do and don't do. We post clever shit on Twitter and Facebook so people will think we're good and love us. We lie to people about whether or not we've seen movies and read books so that they will love us. We date unrepentant assholes and stay with them long after they've proven they bring nothing but misery and emotional bloodshed into our lives because we think they might still somehow qualify as a source of love, however polluted, and that if we leave them, we will be permanently forsaken. We treat every opportunity for love as though it were the last train leaving the station. If we don't get on this one, and quickly, how long and how lonely is the night ahead?

Living this way, with the belief that every chance was my last chance to do something awesome and get the love I needed, had the paradoxical effect of making me a pretty thorough loser. My first job out of college, as an education counselor for incarcerated youth, had me so unnerved by the prospect of epic and public failure that I spent about 40 percent of each workday in my office with the door closed chatting on AOL and looking at porn. Whenever my wife told me that something I had done had been hurtful to her, no matter how minor, I would fly into a low-grade, palm-sweating panic and start constructing any cockamamie argument I could assemble out of discarded shards of truth to prove that *she* was, in fact, the wrong one in the situation. "Yeah, I lied about spending that money on weed, but I wouldn't have to lie if you weren't so judgmental!"

It was not a choice. It was automatic. I couldn't stop it even when I wanted to. A logical part of my brain would say, "Hey, don't you think we're being a little bit ridiculous right now?" But shadowy and powerful forces buried deep within the bedrock of my consciousness would be thundering, "No one loves you! Because you are not perfect! Win this argument now if you want to live!"

It was funny. Until it wasn't. Once I had what seemed at the time like a monumental work task that I feared I wouldn't be able to execute with the perfection required to win me universal adoration. So I decided instead that it would be easier if I died. Not ask for help. Not tell my team I'm struggling and see if they had any advice. Not just let myself fail. Just *die* was my best plan. Literally, I thought, *Well, if I died, then this would all be sorted out.* That thought came to me on a Tuesday afternoon and stayed with me for almost two years.

I was the kind of person who would rather die than ask for help.

And then I lost everything. My wife left me, having put up with more than enough of my shit. Because I had half-assed my career, on the basis that a full-assing carried with it the risk of a full failure, my money situation was effectively a joke. I didn't have a place to live. I hit a kind of bottom that I hope never to repeat. And instead of looking for reasons why it was everyone else's fault, I finally started to ask myself, *Dude. What happened?* But asking myself that wasn't the thing that helped. If I could have answered that question, then I wouldn't have had the problem in the first place. A problem can't be solved by the same brain that created it, no matter how many come-to-Jesus moments that brain thinks it has. Things really started to get right when I asked other people, older people, people more experienced than I, people whose lives were going infinitely better than mine, "What do *you* think happened?" And for the first time in my life, the pain I was in was so great, so insurmountable, and so unconditionally devastating, that I was willing to admit that I needed help. And I was willing to take it. For the first time in my life, I was willing to listen.

And people told me. "Well, you're fine. You're just self-centered. You have been hurtful to some people who have loved you, and you need to make that right. You need to get honest about your fears. You need to forgive yourself for your fears. You need to recognize that your fears, while powerful, are just tricks of your imagination. You need to prioritize doing what's right, what's loving, what's responsible, and what's necessary over your fears. And you need to recognize that you are enough. Even as you struggle, grow, mess up, make mistakes, get overwhelmed, and occasionally do things completely wrong, you are still enough. You are still worthy of love. Not everyone's love, but your own love.

You are worthy of your own love.

And here's the thing: when you have a decent supply of your own love, then you stop putting undue pressure on everyone else to give you theirs. Which, of course, makes you much easier to love.

So if I could go back to that self-obsessed, deeply uncomfortable, AOL-chatting, responsibility-dodging, weed-smoking, wildly insecure person that I was at age twenty-two, I would say to him, "Hey. It's okay that you feel all wrong. Because you're all right. Now get back to work. And ask for help."

L Is For . . .

➤➤

LAUREN WACHENFELD

L is for *Lauren*. *L* is also for *lesbian*. My story started my freshman year of high school, when my friend Morgan and I spent our summer days roaming around Europe together and our nights talking about our hopes and dreams until speckles of pink began to appear in the sky. I didn't yet know what it meant that I always wanted our hugs to last longer, our talks to go deeper. That relationship kicked off a five-year-long battle against the growing realization that the boys I was dating would never be right for me.

Going to college completely changed who I thought I was. Being in such a liberal environment made me realize that it was okay to be a girl who likes girls. I was accepted by (almost) everyone, something I wasn't used to back home in my conservative town in Ohio. I eventually came out to all of my friends and family, began a long-term relationship, ended a long-term relationship, accepted my sexuality, and graduated. Just as I was feeling comfortable in my own skin, I left my liberal college bubble of St. Louis and moved to a more conservative area in Kentucky for work.

One great thing about college that I wasn't always conscious of is that you are constantly surrounded by people your age. I definitely took that for granted, as I am now the youngest person at my new job. Honestly, I am not sure how to meet people after college. Especially when the LGBT pool is so much smaller. I wanted companionship. I wanted romance. I wanted love. So naturally, I signed up for Tinder and HER, two dating apps that have become the norm for us millennials. I should have known what would happen next.

The first little icon that appeared for me showed a picture of a twenty-one-year-old girl in a baseball hat. Okay, decent, so I clicked to learn more about her: "Fun couple looking for a third to mess around with." Looking at more pictures, they were of a shirtless guy (face not shown, because why would that matter, right?) and a girl's chest.

Swipe.

The next girl looked way too young to be twenty-two, as her age listed. Sure enough, her bio proudly proclaimed: "I'm 16, not 22. No haterz."

Swipe.

The next girl had a bio that was basically a novel of emojis, from which I gathered that cannabis was the biggest part of her life, she identified as a Wiccan, and adamantly hated mind games. All of which is fine, just not up my particular alley.

Swipe.

Swiping over and over again became exhausting, and from my very rigorous research, I guessed the following statistics for why people in Kentucky were on lesbian dating apps: 59 percent looking for a third, 10 percent lying about their age to experiment, 16 percent just trying to get swipes based on their bodies, and 3 percent trying to get over a recent breakup, which leaves 12 percent of viable options to try to connect with. And to be honest, I probably fell within those last two categories. The search was like when you go to a clearance sale and have to try to dig through bins upon bins of badly sequined or awkwardly shaped clothes to find that one top that was worth the two-hour search because of the 80 percent off price. Needless to say, this introvert was exhausted.

I took some time off from the virtual world to experience the real world (crazy, I know) and decided to see if going to a gay bar was any better.

I was visiting Columbus, Ohio, a few nights after the massacre at an LGBT club in Orlando, and my friends and I decided to go to a gay bar. It was packed. It felt so good to be in a space with people who were like me and people who would understand the painful emotions I was feeling after the shooting. We danced and laughed and let the music rule. About an hour in, I found myself dancing with a friend of a friend. In the time it took Missy Elliott to rap her lines in "Lose Control," this girl and I had started making out on the dance floor. I thought to myself, *Hmm, I guess this is how you meet people after college.*

When I returned to Kentucky, my dance-floor makeout turned into my texting buddy for a couple of weeks, then turned into that person whose Snapchat story you watch every other week or so. And life went on.

I think the hardest part about meeting people in most public spaces is that you can't always tell who is gay, and you can't always tell where it's okay to be yourself. My mom sat me down before I started my job and warned me not to talk about my nonheterosexual status at work, at least until I had been there awhile and was established. It felt crazy to me that I would have to hide who I was, especially since I had come so far in accepting myself. It also makes it that much harder to meet girls if I have to retreat back into the closet. Sometimes I wish I had a sign that I could carry into straight bars that said, "Hi! I'm gay and would like to get to know you better!" but really that's not practical. Regardless, I still haven't nailed down how to meet and maintain relationships with gay people postgrad. Each experience gets me a little bit closer and allows me to be a little more comfortable with where I am, though I am still figuring out how to fit into the letters of an ever-growing acronym. *L* may stand for *Lauren* and for *lesbian*. But ultimately, *L* is for *learning*.

Why I Want to Live Like I'm Forty In My Twenties

ASHLEY FORD

My best friend and I are both named Ashley, we're both twenty-eight years old (born twelve days apart), and we both have brown eyes. That is pretty much where our similarities end. She loves animal print, high heels, Channing Tatum, and holding on to the hope that she looks this young (or younger) forever. I love tartan, Converse, and Idris Elba.

I also love aging.

In my mind, every year of my life is an opportunity to learn more about who I am and what I want from this life. It also gets me closer to the age I've always wanted to be . . . forty.

I'll be honest, watching the years tick by, another scratch on the wall, hasn't always been a source of pleasure for me. When I entered college, I assumed I would graduate in four years just like I was supposed to, the way we all were supposed to. Being the control freak I am, I'd studied my course catalog all summer, drawing my own charts until I was satisfied that I had a foolproof plan for getting out of school in a respectable amount of time. And that was really what I wanted so badly: to be re-spected.

I ended up changing majors seven times, and along with my perfect guide to on-time graduation, my dream of being "the one who did it right" flew right out the window. I was obsessed with the fact that I would be twenty-three when I graduated college. Then, something else happened, and I would be twenty-four when I graduated college. I didn't leave the uni-versity until I was twenty-five, and did so quietly with a head hung in shame. Someone said, "Ashley, you can't leave! You're like our leader here. Like an old, wise matriarch." I kept pack-ing my boxes and thought, *You got the "old" part right.*

Over coffee, I talked to one of my mentors about my frus-tration with the trajectory of my life. I'd gotten over feeling old, but I still felt stuck. She was everything I wanted to be. A successful writer, honest, warm, and what I like to call "fuck-less." "Fuckless" being the state of giving few, if any, fucks about what others think of you or what you choose to do. It's not about apathy as much as it is a certainty about who you are and what you're meant to do in this world. I saw that in her, and I wanted to live that way as well, with confidence and a sure stride. I wanted to say what I meant and do what felt right. When I told her as much, she responded, "Honey, you'll be the same way when you're forty. This is what happens to all women when we turn forty." We laughed and continued sip-ping our coffee and talking MFAs, publishing, and lit scene gossip. Through it all, there was a clear thought in the back of my head: *I don't want to wait until I'm forty.*

Over the next year, the circumstances of my life changed dramatically. I started dating the love of my life, landed my dream job, and moved to New York City. It felt like when I told people my age and what I was doing with my life, the two sounded like a match. Finally, I was "the one doing it right." I still didn't feel any better about myself. I felt accomplished, I felt capable, and I felt lucky. But the fact that I was where I was "supposed" to be and people could see that now didn't come with the sigh of relief and satisfaction I thought it would. I realized I was waiting for someone to say, "You've done great, Ashley. Now, go live the life you want, and we'll stop watching you." It took me a long time to realize that's not how it works. No one was coming to give me permission to live like I'm forty. I didn't need their permission.

Zora Neale Hurston wrote that there are "years that ask questions and years that answer them." At the top of my third year out of college, I asked myself what was keeping me from living like the forty-year-old women I love, respect, and admire. Aside from some arbitrary assertion that I had not paid my dues or lived enough years, why was I holding myself back from saying what I mean and asking for what I want? Who was I waiting on to give me permission to be me? My answer to myself was that life is too short to wait, and wanting to be forty was never about aging. It was always about wanting to embrace a certain state of mind. I've decided that time is now. I asked the question, and I gave myself permission to answer it, too. Now, I go to seek a great fucklessness.

Not Just Four Walls and a Roof

CAMERON SUMMERS

When I moved back home after college, my room was almost exactly as I had left it four years ago. Unfortunately, so was my family.

I guess I didn't know what to expect when I came home. Would my time away have given my dad the chance to work on some things? It wasn't like Mom had forgotten to update me on his mood swings from time to time. When I was under the bell tower, he was overreacting. When I was walking to the dining hall, he was running out of new curses to use. Strangely, when I came back home, things were initially happy. But it was a honeymoon phase. A few days came and went before it was back to the same old: waking up to cupboards slamming, dishes clanging, yelling. I envied my brother. He moved to California after he graduated. He had a knack for knowing when to get out.

I found out just shy of my first Christmas back home that Mom and Dad were getting a divorce. Some people say it's easier when you're older and this happens, because you're old enough to understand the situation better. I can say from experience, it's still not easy. It was bizarre. When you get to be in your twenties, you start seeing your parents as other people. They're not just Mom or Dad anymore. They're a fifty-nine-year-old man who hasn't been happy for years and a mother of two who just wants her sons to have a good life. It racks your head. The only easy thing was my decision to stay home and take care of my mom. And so that is what I did.

The first things that my mom and I did together were things that we could never do when Dad lived at home. He would always turn the radio off if we played it. He got angry if anyone spoke after he went to bed at 9:00 every night. And he hated candles. He would just blow them out. And so Mom and I cranked up the radio and conversed long past midnight. The day that the divorce was finalized, I gave my mom a special gift that I had been saving for her.

It was a scented candle. It only cost nine dollars, but it meant the world to my mom. She kept on saying that it was like she had been robbed, like years of her life were gone, but I like to think that the candle gave her hope. Her life was not over. She had a new beginning. We sat and lit the candle together in the same spot she had broken the news of the divorce to me. We danced and sang. Days came and went, and we were happier than we had ever been before. We did things to restore the house that my dad had built in the late '80s. Yes, this was the house that he built and the home that he hurt. But my mom and I were going to make it like new.

There came, of course, responsibilities with this freedom. Even though I became frustrated and impatient from time to time, I did my best to look after my mom. I talked things out with her. I helped around the house. I helped her take care of herself. My mom had always been there for me. She had always been my rock. And for four years, when I was gone at school, she stayed that way. Coming back to the home that I had left her in, I knew I had to help restore her happiness and be there to be her advocate. She had done those things for me.

To me, she has always been my mom. But she was once like me. A young person who, in wanting to live life like her parents had done, and theirs before them, got married and started a family. And I had to see that. I had to see the trials my mom had gone through. Coming back home after school gave me that chance. I had the unique opportunity to get closer to her through a personal struggle. I got to be a better son and help her just as she had, for all my life, helped me. We began a brighter future together after some dark times, and we moved forward. There was still uncertainty. But I never doubted my decision to stay at home with my mom. Helping take care of her made me realize that my own life was going someplace better. At some point in watching the flick of fire in that first scented candle and the light it brought to my mother's eyes, I was a new person altogether. I was reborn.

How to Make New Friends as an Adult and Why

PUJA PATEL

When I was growing up, my best friends were simply the ones most available to me. That's true for
most of us, probably—even if we don't realize it
at the time. My next-door neighbor Miranda was my closest
childhood confidant: She was the cooler, older girl who pretended to be witches with me when we were children, lent me
her velour top for the middle school dance, and taught a teen-
aged me about Alanis Morissette and Fiona Apple and alt-girl
angst. She and her art school friends compelled me to read books
I probably didn't understand, and one of them convinced me
I was a socialist at the tender age of fourteen. Miranda and I
kept in touch when she went away to college, but our contact
dwindled once I moved away to go to school myself. She got
married soon after, at an age where I was still trying to master
flirting with boys. Now I see photos of her four kids on Instagram and "like" every one of them. I can tell from the pictures
that I'd probably get along with her middle daughter the best—
she seems to be the most like her mom when she was a kid.

And that's how it goes, doesn't it? Until you're capable of

making decisions for yourself—or wise enough to be able to tell the difference between legitimate shared interests and mere tipsy camaraderie or friendly groupthink—most of the friends you make before your mid-to late twenties just happen to be the most convenient. The neighbors close enough for your parents to keep an eye on, the classmates most tolerant of your beautiful adolescent bullshit, and the college-dorm and first-job cohorts who'd inevitably witness your first steps into adulthood. These people are important, they're your friends, they saw you through Some Shit. They may also not be around anymore.

Yes, meeting new people gets harder as you get older—sometimes the mere idea can send a person into an existential crisis. But the friends you make as adults tend to bond to you much faster, if only because you're all quicker to embrace your own quirks and have (hopefully) become more self-aware about who you can tolerate. Being clear-eyed about that sort of thing is half the battle. Here's some advice on how to make it through the other half.

It's okay to let go of some people to make room for new ones. At the risk of sounding callous, there are times when older relationships can get to be more trouble than they're worth. The upside is that you might find that you're more willing to open yourself up to new people than before. (It isn't so different from dating, to be honest.) It's easy for some to detach from those who're getting them down, but often, the familiarity/comfort makes it too damn hard. But consider reevaluating the following:

- The friends you may not vibe with, but are wrapped up in routine: You've always watched the Big Game with them, and you always will . . . even though you hate their politics, and their girlfriend, and their house, and the way they make you feel like crap about the fact that your life does not remotely resemble theirs. Perhaps you could try watching the next Big Game somewhere else?

• The boors whose loud opinions you can't stomach anymore: Facebook is evil and abrasive and yet, somehow, a great way to determine whether you ever want to talk to someone ever again. When you log in and see that your old high school pal shared the BuzzFeed post "Lena Dunham's New Podcast Proves That She's the World's Greatest Feminist"—with the added caption "YAAAAAS QUEEEN"—or your old college drinking buddy is suddenly very interested in building walls and Making America Great Again, it might be time to cite irreconcilable differences on the subjects of life, liberty, and general good taste. By all means, be tolerant of differing opinions, but also accept when you've been confronted with an unavoidable deal breaker.

• The constant catcher-uppers: These are particularly difficult to navigate—the ones where you keep having the same empty con- versations. All of your text messages involve an innocuous prom- ise to "catch up soon!" that involves listing things that can be readily discovered about you on the Internet, in lieu of expanding on them or talking about anything real at all. (To be fair, it's hard to talk about real things with people you rarely speak to.) Or when the only common ground you have anymore involves past events now so distant that you've hashed them out to completion.

God, it sounds petty, doesn't it? It feels worse! But, man, it's cool to lean into your own sanity from time to time. You don't need to break up with anyone outright, but it couldn't hurt to, y'know, see other people.

You might feel out of touch with close friends, too. But they're not going anywhere. "Make new friends, but keep the old," they say, and even then, it's painful to feel a great distance with your closest friends. These are the lifers—the ones who've seen you at your best (and your worst), and perhaps barely see you at all anymore. It feels like the death of something— your #squad! your youth!—but they helped make you who you are today, and you'll still turn to each other in your most trying hours. And it's okay to want to experience new things with new people who can better appreciate the new (and hopefully improved) you. But how do you meet those people?

Do what you actually want to be doing. All this talk of change means looking inward, too. What do you want to change about the way you spend your time? What would you be doing if you had a pal to do it with? Want to join a rec league or play pickup basketball with the guys at your neighborhood court? Looking to take a cooking class or join a hobby-oriented club of some kind? Just do it. Writing your name down on that sign-up sheet and introducing yourself to a bunch of strangers with ostensibly similar interests is the hardest part of all this. See a good concert coming up, but can't convince anybody to tag along? Go alone. Maybe you'll spot someone you know, or strike up a convo with the other guy posted up at the bar, singing along to "Shake It Off" between shots of whiskey. You are not a loser; you are an advanced human.

Look at the people around you. Life is very hard and depressing, and staring at the ground is a solid way to avoid direct eye contact with anyone who might want to ask you what did you do this weekend (i.e., Netflix and Chill, but without the sexy part). That said, your coworkers are living under the same confusing overlords and navigating the same workplace dramas on a daily basis, and given that you probably spend more time with them than anyone else these days, you probably don't want for conversation starters. I personally have the advantage of working in a place with preexisting friends, and our jobs largely revolve around shared interests, but shooting the shit (and talking shit) over a drink is still the quickest way to find out whether you've got chemistry outside the walls of your shared prison. (Note: Don't get too drunk or loose-lipped during your first hang. Just revel in the fact that you've both survived another day.)

If you've recently moved or switched career paths, ask your friends to put you in touch with people they know in your new area or new area of expertise. And be open. When you're looking for a job, the rule is supposedly, "Never say no to a meeting," and the same mentality applies here: When a friend-of-a-friend invites you to a group outing or suggests grabbing a drink at a new bar in your neighborhood, you should do them, and yourself, the decency of doing it. (Assuming that your friend's friends aren't total clowns, of course.) Take friendly people up on their offers to hang, as it might have taken them the same minuscule amount of awkward bravery to ask that it will take you to say yes. If you're a parent looking for other parent friends, use your kids as easy bait: find the "cool dad" or "cool mom" in your kid's class or playgroup, make sure their child isn't a lunatic and knows how to share his LEGOs, and then set up a playdate.

Reach out to people you admire. Several of my coworkers have copped to "sliding into the DMs" of someone whose work they admired or whose online personality vibes with their own. If it seems like someone you're friends with online would be up for an IRL conversation about something you're both passionate about, reach out. (Seriously, writers do this all the time!) This may require you to be a little more outgoing than you want to be—you've progressed from approaching strangers with shared hobbies to someone with whom you've friend-crushed on online—but folks who actively engage with others online are usually accustomed to talking to strangers.

Be cool, man. Listen, no one is obligated to be your bestie. Like I said earlier, this whole thing is sort of like dating. It will come with the usual weird gaps in communication, the awkward laughs at not-so-funny jokes, and anxieties on the order of "Why hasn't Cool Tom replied to my invite to see a movie? Am I too weird? Did I accidentally diss him? Am I going to die alone?" As a fully grown adult, you've got to understand that people your own age are very busy and easily tired, *just like you*. Be chill about it. Consider it one more thing you have in common.

I Moved Cross-Country for a Guy

>>«

MYISHA BATTLE

I could say that delusion led me to New York. But what I felt was real. I was not overly confident, but I was in love, and I trusted the notion that if things didn't work out, we'd discuss it like two grown-ups and move on. I made a plan, and I thought I was prepared to fail.

I met him when I was still in college. I was working at an after-school program in Oakland where he was an intern. On certain days, our schedules would overlap, and I'd see him escorting his second-grade class around the school. He was a few years older than I, but when we began talking, we learned we had a lot in common. Music, movies, books—we were almost always in agreement about what was good and what made it so. We started hanging out together outside of work with colleagues but would find ways to end the night together, talking until we had to awkwardly part ways. He was a writer. He would share his drafts, and I would provide him notes. We went for runs together around Lake Merritt after work. He taught me how to play chess. I was hooked.

During my last semester of college, I studied abroad in

Amsterdam. He came to visit me, and after an amazing visit full of sex, intense conversations, and day trips (both physical and psychedelic), I was sure that at some point we would have to see if a future could develop.

While I was abroad, he moved to New York to pursue a writing career. We maintained a friendship and dated other people in our respective cities. We'd talk about the people we were seeing with a "I wish you were here so I didn't have to do this" tone to the conversation, and sometimes that was explicitly stated. Before heading back to California from Amsterdam, I stopped off in New York City and visited him. In retrospect, that visit was full of red flags, but I was so taken by New York buried in snow that I let myself imagine a life for us together there. It wasn't long after returning home that I hatched a plan to move.

Things started to change in the month leading up to my arrival. We didn't talk as regularly as we used to, and I was becoming nervous that he felt pressure to take care of me when I got there. I reassured him that he was not the only thing drawing me to New York. But no matter what I told him or myself, I was not prepared for what happened when I got to his apartment.

"I met someone," he said. "Last week. I think it's serious. You can still stay here, it's just . . ."

I remember walking out of his apartment into a cold October night, pacing frantically in the street as I called my friend back in California.

"It's over. Can you give me the number of your friend who lives out here? I need a place to stay."

Within a couple of days, I was crashing on a couch in Greenpoint. I started my new job and hunted feverishly for a room to rent. I cried a lot. I didn't sleep well. My stomach was in knots, and my heart was torn.

I could say that delusion led me to New York. But what I felt was real. I never could have predicted how devastating his actions would be. I was twenty-three, had lived on my own in another country, and was already independent, but I had never felt more abandoned than in those first weeks in New York. I could have left immediately. I don't think anyone would have questioned that decision, but it never crossed my mind.

We live in a cultural moment that values rational decision-making even in matters of the heart. When I moved, I felt that the worst thing to do would be to let reason give way to feeling, so I gave everyone around me all of these additional explanations for moving: grad school, new job, needing to escape the West Coast. But the pull of love will always be the real reason I moved. I used to admit that reluctantly as if it were a failure of character, but now I know that enduring heartache taught me the capacity I have to both hurt and be hurt, and that cannot be underestimated.

I have continued to take risks with my heart because I find strength even in failed attempts at love, and I don't want a life full of what-ifs. Desire is not logical, it cannot be planned, and it takes courage to see it through.

You Don't Need More Friends

→》 《←

SCAACHI KOUL

The worst breakups you'll experience in those first few bursts of adulthood—when you move into a real apartment where the radiator doesn't sing or when you clean the fridge for the first time because the rotten vegetable juice at the bottom of the crisper was getting out of control—won't be with people you're dating. There will come a time when you look at your friend, or their name flashes in your mind, and you remember that you're not friends anymore.

It's easy to think, *No, not us, we are the closest friends, we are almost siblings, we feel the world together, we will never let outside forces tear us apart,* but love makes us stupid. It's okay to be stupid. It may take time for this to settle in, but I can wait. I will still be here for you when you realize I'm right.

Some of them will melt rather than crack, that quiet ebb of a relationship that you'll both allow without really noticing. Someone will move, maybe, or you'll start "dating" other people, or you'll get a new job and it'll be harder to go out for drinks or meet for lunch. Some will drive glass into your heart, accusing you of malfeasance or rebellion or disloyalty. Or you'll feel that they did the same to you, and you'll break it apart with your bare hands. Whatever the case: the older you get, the fewer people you'll be able to keep in your pocket.

Sometimes we make friends that feel like good ideas in the moment but turn out to be unbelievable tragedies for ourselves the older we get. That girl who took us to fun bars and showed us how to snort a line off the back of her hand in the bathroom? She was fun, but she was mean, and she'd abandon us in places we didn't feel safe. That guy who made us laugh in class and who, we were sure, we'd keep in touch with once we graduated? Turns out he was a dick to literally everyone else, and we ignored it for so long because we wanted him to be good.

Have I ever told you about my best friend, Baby Braga? I call him that, because when we met, we were seventeen, and I hated him, and he had the smallest body and the biggest head, and I called him a baby because I could. We were only friends because of our mutual friend, a burly blockhead who I loved enough to tolerate this other weeny. Baby Braga and I spent a lot of university together. We went to the same parties, he dated a few of my friends, we liked the same books, the same television shows. Sometimes we'd have lunch together. We went to the movies now and then. I taught him how to cook a chicken breast in an oven.

By the time we graduated, we looked around and noticed that no one else was really there. We'd lost touch with most of the people that pulled us together, we missed almost no one, and that blockhead mutual buddy we had? He assaulted me years prior and was cast away in quick order. It was just us. And who would have predicted that at the core of our social nucleus, the twenty-some people we surrounded ourselves with for years, there would only be the two of us?

Contributor Bios

AARON GILBREATH

Aaron grew up in Phoenix and attended the University of Arizona in Tucson. He's written for *Harper's*, *The New York Times*, *Lucky Peach*, and *The Paris Review*, and is the author of the personal essay collection *Everything We Don't Know*, and *This Is: Essays on Jazz*. He eats tacos in Portland, Oregon.

AILEEN GARCIA

Aileen grew up in Manila, Philippines. She holds a degree in psychology and is currently pursuing her doctoral degree. She lives with her husband in Lincoln, Nebraska.

ALANA MASSEY

Alana Massey grew up wherever the US Navy sent her family before moving to New York City to attend New York University. Her writing regularly appears in *The Guardian*, *Elle*, *New York Magazine*, and more. She is the author of *All The Lives I Want* and a book publishing in 2018 about the value of women's work. She splits her time between Brooklyn and her home in Saugerties, New York.

ALEXANDRA MOLOTKOW

Alexandra Molotkow grew up in Toronto. She went to the University of Toronto. Her writing has appeared in *The Cut*, *The New Republic*, *The Believer*, and *The New York Times Magazine*, and she was a founding editor of *Hazlitt*. She is currently an editor at *Real Life* magazine and lives in New York.

ALISON GILBERT

Alison grew up in Interlaken, New Jersey. She went to the George Washington University. She founded and currently runs Project AG, a business strategy and coaching consultancy that helps emerging entrepreneurs build thriving businesses. She lives in New York City.

ASHLEY FORD

Ashley C. Ford grew up in Fort Wayne, Indiana. She attended Ball State University in Muncie, Indiana (frequently mentioned on *Parks and Recreation*). She is currently a writer and editor living in Brooklyn, New York. She's written for *Elle*, BuzzFeed, *The Guardian*, and more.

BIJAN STEPHEN

Bijan Stephen grew up in Tyler, Texas, and studied biology at Yale University. He's written for *The New York Times Magazine*, *Wired*, *The New Republic*, *The Believer*, and others. He is currently a culture reporter for *Vice News Tonight* on HBO. He lives in Brooklyn, New York.

CAMERON SUMMERS

Cameron grew up in Holly, Michigan. He graduated from the University of Michigan–Ann Arbor. He currently teaches in his hometown of Holly, where he lives.

CARVELL WALLACE

Carvell Wallace grew up moving between small-town Pennsylvania, medium-town D.C., and big-town LA. He attended New York University's Tisch School of the Arts, where he proudly took a degree in something called "experimental theatre." He currently writes for MTV News, *The New Yorker*, *The Guardian*, and others. When he's not writing, he's experiencing overwhelming love for his two occasionally difficult and always beautiful children. Every single day, he asks someone somewhere for help.

CHLOE ANGYAL

Chloe Angyal, Ph.D., is a journalist from Sydney, Australia, who lives in New York City. She is a senior front page editor at *The Huffington Post*. Her writing has been published in *The Washington Post*, *The Atlantic*, and *The New York Times*.

EMILY GOULD

Emily Gould grew up in Silver Spring, Maryland. She attended Kenyon College and graduated from Eugene Lang College. She cofounded emilybooks.com and is the author of a novel, *Friendship*, and an essay collection, *And the Heart Says Whatever*.

ERIC ANTHONY GLOVER

Eric was born in Washington, D.C., and grew up in Wheaton, Maryland. He studied writing at Sarah Lawrence College. Eric is pursuing a career in screenwriting in New York City. He lives in Brooklyn, New York.

GALA MUKOMOLOVA

Gala Mukomolova is a Moscow-born, Brooklyn-raised, NYC writer. She received her MFA from the Helen Zell Writers' Program, and her past residencies include Vermont Studio Center, Six Points Fellowship for

Emerging Jewish Artists, and the Pink Door. Her poems and essays have appeared in numerous publications, such as *Vinyl*, *The James Franco Review*, and *Poetry*. Monthly, she writes poetic horoscopes under the moniker Galactic Rabbit.

JAMIE LAUREN KEILES

Jamie Lauren Keiles grew up in the suburbs of Philadelphia and studied at the University of Chicago. She writes about the messier corners of the digital world and has been published in *The New York Times Magazine* and on *New York*'s *The Cut*, among other places. She currently splits her time between Queens, New York, and Los Angeles.

JASON DIAMOND

Jason Diamond grew up around the Chicagoland area. He went to a few different colleges because variety is the spice of life, is the founder of Vol. 1 Brooklyn, has written for *The New York Times*, *The Paris Review*, and *Vice*, among others, and he's the author of the memoir *Searching for John Hughes*. He lives in Brooklyn, New York.

JENNY ZHANG

Jenny was born in Shanghai and raised in New York. She attended Stanford University and the Iowa Writers' Workshop. She is the author of *Dear Jenny, We Are All Find* and the collection of short stories *Sour Heart* (Random House, Fall 2017). Her work has been published in *The New York Times*, *New York*, *Poetry*, BuzzFeed, and *Rookie*, among other places. She currently lives in Brooklyn, New York.

JUSTIN WARNER

Justin Warner grew up in Hagerstown, Maryland. He bypassed college to begin his career in the food industry and was a captain at Danny Meyer's acclaimed restaurant, the Modern. Justin is the winner of the eighth season of *Food Network Star* and was the chef/co-owner of the Michelin-rated Do or Dine restaurant in Brooklyn before publishing his cookbook *The Laws of Cooking . . . and How to Break Them*. He currently hosts the show *Foodie Call* and lives in Brooklyn, New York.

KEVIN NGUYEN

Kevin was raised in a suburb outside of Boston and went to college at the University of Puget Sound on the opposite side of the country. He has worked at Amazon, Oyster, Google, and is currently an editor at *GQ*. His writing has been published in *The New York Times*, *The New Republic*, *The Paris Review*, *Grantland*, and elsewhere. He currently lives in Brooklyn, New York.

KRISTIN RUSSO

Kristin grew up in upstate New York and attended Binghamton University, Marymount Manhattan College, and the Graduate Center, CUNY. She is the CEO of LGBTQ organizations Everyone Is Gay and My Kid Is Gay and authored *This Is a Book for Parents of Gay Kids* (Chronicle, 2014).

LANE MOORE

Lane grew up in North Carolina. *Paste Magazine* called her the 19th Funniest Person on Twitter, *Brooklyn Magazine* named her one of the 50 Funniest People in Brooklyn, and *BUST Magazine* named her one of 10 Funny Ladies You Need To Be Watching. She is the creator and host of the critically acclaimed comedy show *Tinder Live* and has guest starred on HBO's *Girls*. She has written for *The New Yorker*, *The Onion*, *McSweeney's*, and *GQ. BUST Magazine* called her band It Was Romance "The Best Band of 2015." She lives in New York City.

LAURA WILLCOX

Laura grew up in Montclair, New Jersey, and attended Tufts University. She is a longtime writer/performer at the Upright Citizens Brigade Theatre in New York City. Laura has appeared on *Inside Amy Schumer*, *Late Night with Seth Meyers*, MTV's *Hey Girl*, and several national commercials and has written for shows like MTV's *Girl Code* and *Alec Baldwin's Love Ride* for TruTV. Her parody wedding guidebook, *I Am Bride: How to Take the "We" Out of Wedding (And Other Useful Advice)* was published January 2017 by Abrams Books. She currently lives in Los Angeles, California.

LAUREN WACHENFELD

Lauren grew up in Loveland, Ohio. She went to Washington University in St. Louis. She currently works at Wild Flavors as a Beverage Lab Technician. She hopes to become a Flavor Chemist, while maintaining her love for writing and music on the side. She lives in Cincinnati, Ohio.

LINCOLN BLADES

Lincoln grew up in Toronto and has lived everywhere from Barbados to Montreal. He went to York University. He currently is a freelance writer, a blogger for ThisIsYourConscience.com, and host of the news program *All Things Being Equal*. He currently lives in Toronto, Canada.

LORI ADELMAN

Lori was born in Philadelphia and raised in New Jersey. She attended Harvard College, where she studied social sciences. She is currently the Director of Global Communications at Planned Parenthood Global and runs the popular website Feministing.com. She lives in Brooklyn, New York.

MARA WILSON

Mara Wilson grew up in Burbank, California, where she worked as a child actress in such films as *Mrs. Doubtfire* and *Matilda* before moving to New York to attend New York University. She is the author of the book *Where Am I Now?* as well as the host of the storytelling show *What Are You Afraid Of?* Mara lives in New York City.

MIRA GONZALEZ

Mira Gonzalez grew up in Venice Beach, California. She went to Santa Monica College, where she studied child psychology. She is the author of two books: *I Will Never Be Beautiful Enough to Make Us Beautiful Together* (Sorry House, 2013) and *Selected Tweets* (Hobart, 2015). She currently lives in Los Angeles with her Pomeranian, Parsnip.

MOLLY SODA

Molly Soda was born in San Juan, Puerto Rico, and grew up in Bloomington, Indiana. She went to Tisch School of the Arts at New York University. She currently works for herself, sharing her work online and exhibiting in shows around the world. She lives in New York.

MYISHA BATTLE

Myisha grew up in Shreveport, Louisiana. She went to San Francisco State University and the New School. She is currently a sex coach and hosts the sex-positive podcast *Down for Whatever*. She lives in San Francisco, California.

NIA KING

Nia King is a queer, mixed Black art activist from Canton, Massachusetts. She is the author of *Queer & Trans Artists of Color: Stories of Some of Our Lives* and the host and producer of *We Want the Airwaves* podcast. Her writing has been published in *East Bay Express*, *Women & Performance: a journal of feminist theory*, and *make/shift* magazine. She graduated from Mills College in 2011 and lives in Oakland, California.

NISHA BHAT

Nisha grew up around the Pittsburgh, PA, area and went to the University of Pittsburgh where she earned a B.S. in economics and neuroscience. She works in the healthcare IT industry as a Consulting Analyst with Cerner Corporation. She resides in the Philadelphia area.

PAULETTE PERHACH

Paulette Perhach is a writer living in Seattle, Washington. She grew up on the Gulf Coast and earned her magazine journalism degree from the University of Florida. She has worked for various magazines and newspapers and is the creator of the Writer's Welcome Kit, an e-course for new writers on how to get started, which is offered through and benefits the nonprofit Hugo House, a Seattle writing center. A printed version will be published in 2018 by Sasquatch Books. Her work has appeared in *The New York Times*, *Elle*, *Marie Claire*, *Salon*, *The Journal*, and *The Huffington Post*.

PUJA PATEL

Puja Patel is a writer and editor who grew up outside of Baltimore, Maryland. She is currently an editor at *Deadspin*, where she oversees their culture and lifestyle coverage. She lives in Brooklyn, New York.

SAM ZABELL

Sam grew up in Cleveland, Ohio, and attended the Medill School of Journalism at Northwestern University. She's currently an editor at *Real Simple* and hosts the podcast *Adulthood Made Easy*. She lives in New York City.

SARAH MIRK

Sarah Mirk is a multimedia journalist based in Portland, Oregon, who is always curious about gender, politics, and identity. She's the online editor of feminism and pop culture nonprofit Bitch Media and the host the feminist podcast *Popaganda*. In 2014, she published the open-minded relationship book *Sex from Scratch: Making Your Own Relationship Rules*.

SCAACHI KOUL

Scaachi grew up in Calgary, Alberta. She went to Ryerson University for journalism. She's currently a senior writer for BuzzFeed, and her debut collection of essays is *One Day We'll All Be Dead and None of This Will Matter* (Picador, Spring 2017). She lives in Toronto, Ontario.

SHANNON KEATING

Shannon grew up in Ridgefield, Connecticut. She went to Connecticut College. Her writing has been published in/on TheAtlantic.com, *Salon*, The Hairpin, *Jezebel*, *The Rumpus*, *Bitch*, and others. She's currently the LGBT editor at BuzzFeed and lives in New York City.

SKYLAR KERGIL

Skylar Kergil grew up in Acton, Massachusetts. He graduated from Skidmore College in 2013. He currently travels nationally to share his story about transitioning from female to male at seventeen and provide resources for the transgender community and allies. He lives in Boston where he writes music.

WHITNEY MIXTER

Whitney Mixter grew up in Connecticut and attended Pace University in NYC. She is best known for her role on Showtime's *The Real L Word* and VH1's *Couples Therapy*. She currently resides in Los Angeles, where she is an event producer, actress, and media commentator.

Acknowledgments

Thank you especially to Bryn Clark, Kara Rota, and Will Schwalbe and everyone at Flatiron Books for leading the charge in giving students and young professionals a voice.

A special shout out also goes to Alex and Aaron from the MindSumo team who ensured this work became a reality. Their organization and execution moved us forward even before we knew where this project was headed.

Finally, I must acknowledge the authors who have boldly shared their personal stories and perspectives. Your experiences will give others confidence in knowing they are not alone in this stage of life. Thank you for being so real.

—TH

Copyright Acknowledgments